A Passion for Sailing

A Passion for Sailing

With
Cynthia Walker and
Douglas Walker

Bruce W. Walker

Lakehouse Publishing

Published by Lakehouse Publishing

Lake Macquarie NSW, Australia

© Text: Bruce W. Walker Dec. 2021, Cynthia Walker, Douglas Walker

© Illustrations: Bruce W. Walker

The rights of Bruce W. Walker as author of this work are asserted. Apart from use as permitted under the Australian Copyright Act of 1968, no part of this book may be reproduced by any means without prior written permission of the author.

ISBN Print: 9780648497691

ISBN ebook: 9780645332308

A catalogue record for this book is available from the National Library of Australia

Printed in Melbourne, Australia.

Author's contact: brucewwalker@hotmail.com

Free download by https://usedtotech.com

Dedication

To all those sailors and writers who have
provided knowledge and inspiration
and
To my grandchildren who are the future:
Meilah, Annabella, Henley, Neve and Flynn

Contents

Introduction	1
Amateur Yacht Designer and Builder	5
Aragunnu's first cruise	17
Christmas Cruise 1985/6	25
To the South Pacific	27
Aragunnu in the Kingdom of Tonga	35
Aragunnu in Fiji	41
Aragunnu in NZ	47
Doug's journal (Douglas Walker)	55
Island of Dreaming	69
A quiet little cruise	73
Gabo Island	75
Grounding	79
Aground Again	83
The Magician of the Swatchways	85
Iota	89
Navigation	91
Self Steering	95
Harry Pigeon	97
Owning a cruising yacht	101
The Last Hero -Tilman	103
Impressions of Turkey and the Greek Isles	107
More reminiscences of an amateur yacht designer	111
Barnacles on Propellers	113
Lord Howe Island 1994 (Cynthia Walker)	115
Hard Dinghies	121
A Revolution in the Coastal Cruising Club	123

Charles Herbert Lightoller	129
Swansea Rescue	131
Sculling	135
On Communications in the 1990s	137
Some more reminisces	139
Arthur Ransome	143
Lord Howe Island – Tips for Visiting	147
A Little Tender Behind	151
Revolution to Lord Howe Island	153
The Aborted Voyage	157
A Skippered yacht charter – Ionian Isles	161
Our Friends, Greg and Anne Coonan	167
Anatomy of a cruising yacht	175
About the author	197
Acknowledgements	199

Illustrations

Aeolus – Our Southerly 23	2
Bruce, Cynthia and Sue Morley on *Aeolus* (photo: Malcolm Morley)	5
First line drawing	8
Model from first lines	8
Final lines drawing	9
C Flex lay-up showing scaffolding	10
Upturned hull with some moulds removed	10
The hull faring is complete	11
The deck is painted	12
Fitting out – main cabin	13
Bruce fitting out the interior (photo Jim Kelly)	13
Our shed gives birth – *Aragunnu* is lifted onto the loader	18
Launching day, Bermagui Dec. 1982	19
Wetting the keel (Photo Jim Kelly)	19
Inserting 1000lb lead ballast (Photo Jim Kelly)	20
Aragunnu in Sydney Harbour – no bowsprit yet	23
Mainsheet cover Feb 1986 – Christmas Cruises	25
Aragunnu as she was before we went to the South Pacific	27
Nanook and *Aragunnu* at Lord Howe Island 1984	29
Aragunnu closes Vav'u, Tonga (Photo – Greg Coonan)	33
Aragunnu at anchor Port Maurelle	38
Beachcomber, Fiji 1986	43
Walker family aboard Aragunnu at Yanutha I.	44
The Coonans and Walkers, Yasawa Is. Fiji 1986	45
Col y Suva swimming hole	62
Aragunnu with new fibreglass dodger	68
Aragunnu departing Lord Howe Island (Photo Jan Mitchell)	71
Mainsheet Cover – Easter 1988	72

Aragunnu closing on Bermagui (Photo Graham Solomon)	76
Walker family in front of shed where we built *Aragunnu*	77
Sunset at Montague Roads, Gabo I.	78
Drawing – Grounding	79
Drawing – The committee retired at the AGM	82
Drawing – The Commodore's Dinner	88
Drawing – The committee accepted a nomination from the floor	94
Uses for a cat on a yacht – auxiliary propulsion	96
Seabird Yawl in Bermagui Harbour	98
Seagoer Yawl in Bermagui Harbour	99
Harold William Tilman (photo: Wikicommons)	105
Drawing – The Commodore's treasure hunt	106
Uses for a cat – When supplies run low (Cynthia Walker)	110
Balls Pyramid	118
Fleetwood Dingy folded	122
Fleetwood Dinghy ready to go	122
Aragunnu as sold to David Lewis	123
Revolution under sail	125
Revolution on her mooring, Bedlam Bay, Sydney	126
Revolution awaits her new engine	127
Revolution at speed	132
Drawing – Insurance and liability	134
Drawing – The CCC breaks ties with the YA	136
David Lewis under the dodger on Southern Seas (Photo: Dave Hoyle)	139
Southern Seas II in Samoa (Photo Dave Hoyle)	140
Southern Seas undergoing restoration in Kettering	141
Southern Seas II after restoration, Kettering	141
Pom Pom suffers floods in the Richmond River	150
Mounts Lidgebird and Gower looking SSW across the lagoon	147
The crew – Doug, Kerryn and Brian at base of Mt Gower	155
View of the lagoon from Mt Gower	155
Shawfire being craned out of backyard, Gladesville	157
Wayworld 45, *Shawfire,* being launched at River Quays, Parramatta River	159
Ripple Effect	162
Gaia Harbour, Paxos	163
Uses for a cat – as a fender	165

Greg Coonan, Bruce Walker, Anne Coonan and Cynthia Walker	167
Aragunnu rafted alongside *Harmony* in Fame Cove	168
Drawing Greg Coonan overboard in mid Tasman –	167
Aragunnu sailing in Pittwater	176
Drawing – sailing downwind "Goose-winged"	181
Uses for a cat - Decoking exhaust	188
The Author, Bruce W. Walker	197

Introduction

*If a man does not keep pace with his companions
perhaps it is because he hears a different drummer
Let him step to the music which he hears
Henry David Thoreau*

The idea of my owning a boat seemed to arrive at a pretty early age. I don't remember when. Sometime in my late teens, my father announced that he was going to build a boat. He bought some catalogues. These I pawed over for hours. I still have them.

In 1967 at age twenty, I met a tall, feisty, adventurous, extroverted lady named Cynthia. We started going out around the time of my twenty-first birthday and were married three and a half years later. It was to be a lifelong partnership.

I chose a seven-foot hard-chine plywood dinghy as my first building project. Cynthia seemed quite happy to go along with my projects and work proceeded during university holidays.

This was the first of a number of dinghies powered by outboards and oars that I made. In 1974, after a stint teaching in the country and, now married to Cynthia, we agreed to the purchase of a 23-foot fibreglass yacht - a Southerly 23 which we named *Aeolus*. We launched it in Kogarah Bay. With the builders aboard, we sailed it up to Sydney Harbour.

I was, by now, buying every magazine available and studying every aspect of sailing. My life was consumed by it all. There were a couple of changes of career but, by the start of 1976, I had decided to build a yacht and bought plans. I organised to buy a male mould from a fellow who was building one to the same design at Blackwattle Bay. But at the end of 1976, I knew I would be taking a country appointment in my new profession and Cynthia was pregnant with our first child. So in early 1977, we went to Bega, on the far south coast of New South Wales, with our new baby son. We sold *Aeolus* and after a year bought some acreage and built a kit house. By now, I had decided to design and build my own boat. More on that later.

Two more children were born during our six year sojourn in Bega and my vessel, named Aragunnu, was launched in December 1982. We sailed her up the coast to Sydney in January 1983 so I could take up a new appointment in Sydney.

Aeolus, Southerly 23, our first Yacht

Our friends, Greg and Ann Coonan, were similarly inspired and also having re-located to Sydney, bought their first yacht after coming aboard Aragunnu at Easter. We were introduced to the Coastal Cruising Club of Australia Inc. and became members in 1984. In the ensuing years, I took the positions of Cruising Officer, Mainsheet Editor (the monthly journal of the CCC of A), Vice Commodore and Commodore. Much of the material in this anthology featured in The Mainsheet over a twenty year period. As all the articles that follow were written over more than 35 years there is, inevitably, a little repetition. For this I apologise.

I wrote my article, Anatomy of a Cruising Yacht, for the first Coastal Cruising Club of Australia website set up by Doug Inall in 2000/2001. The article was aimed at helping the novice choose a cruising yacht. Some of the information is probably outdated by now, but in general, most still holds true.

We took our cat aboard on one of our weekend sails and had some excitement when a southerly buster blew through the anchored fleet. I thought I had a good relationship with our cat but, during the fracas, he urinated on my pillow and then hid in the engine bay so, by way of revenge, I started a series in The Mainsheet called Uses for a Cat on a Yacht. Members produced drawings with ideas. Four of my sketches are included in this book.

During my time as Editor of The Mainsheet, I drew a number of illustrations for the cover. Some were attempts at humour, some topical. A number of these are also included below.

I have also included four vignettes of some fascinating and intriguing characters from the world of sailing that originally appeared as book reviews in The Mainsheet.

Our children grew up and took up sailing in their teen years. We sold *Aragunnu* and a number of yachts followed (*Revolution, Top Knot, Waituri* and *Mako*). Our youngest daughter, Jane, became interested in competitive sailing with the Drummoyne Twilight Races and three of my yachts were campaigned from 2009 to the present, culminating in our winning our division in the 2020/2021 series.

These are the stories and articles from my yachting years.

In 2013 I was named in the New Years' Honours List for the Principality of Hutt River. In 2015 at Naan, the capital of the Principality, I was inducted by the Late Prince Leonard and became Sir Bruce Walker, Knight Commander of the Order of Wisdom and Learning. Cynthia became entitled to be addressed as Lady Cynthia Walker. But that's a story for another chapter in my life.

Bruce Walker, 2021

Amateur Yacht Designer and Builder
The Bruce Walker Story

In forty years of yacht ownership, *Mako* is my sixth yacht. My wife Cynthia and I started out in 1974 with the purchase of a new Southerly 23, which was featured at the Sydney Boat Show that year. As a reward for allowing my boat to be exhibited, I received some free extras. At that stage, I was reading everything about boats, yachts and sailing that I could lay my hands on and knew a lot about it, but had virtually no hands on experience. My brother and I had looked at an older timber yacht built at Mona Vale, but the survey revealed expensive work needed to be done and we backed out.

Cynthia a friend and Bruce in cockpit *Aeolus* (Southerly 23) – (Photo Malcolm Morley)

That first period of ownership was a very steep learning curve and it was some time before Cynthia had me speaking in plain English instead of the yacht jargon that I had become accustomed to.

We sailed up to Broken Bay quite a few times and I wrote a small article for Australian Boating magazine about beginning ownership for which I received $30. Although young and flexible in our bodies, staying aboard in the confines of a 23' yacht soon had us wishing for something larger. I was in contact with people who were building yachts on the Glebe waterfront (now Glebe High School) and decided that I could build my own. How hard could it be? C-Flex was all the rage at the time (circa 1976) and a fellow offered to sell me his male moulds for a Roberts 32 when he had finished with them. So I purchased C-Flex and the plans for a Roberts 32 which seemed about the right size and, with a full keel, seemed a healthy and safe style of vessel.

Of all the delusions in life, perhaps the most prevalent one is the time it takes to build a yacht. Just ask Greg Coonan how long it took to build his trimaran and how long he thought it would take when he started. The Pardeys were rather more realistic when they wrote that professional yacht builders give a quote based on 1000 hours per tonne of displacement. So a four ton yacht would take 4000 hours which translates into 40 hour weeks for a fifty week year meaning two years for one man working full time in the building. Part time work extends the building, and quality of finish can either extend or decrease the building time. The hull itself takes around one quarter to one seventh of the building time and around one fifth of the cost of materials. Hiring moulds for GRP construction reduces building time. I once met a man who had built a superb ferro cement hull, faultlessly painted green with a sharp red boot topping. I commented on what a beautiful job he had done, admiring the empty hull. I asked how long he had worked on it. He replied, 'Sixteen years.' At that rate he wouldn't live long enough to finish it.

Time was running out for me as I was in a training course for a new job which entailed a posting to the country and the R32 moulds would not be available in time to do a basic lay-up, so I had to back out of that.

I started to get the idea that I might be able to design my own yacht. I hadn't found any designs that I thought might be relatively easy to build and suit my requirements without being too expensive, and I looked at a lot. I was influenced by the Pardeys and their "Go small, go simple, go now" philosophy and I focussed on what I thought would be the smallest sized yacht that would fulfil my requirements, e.g. standing headroom, separate toilet, diesel engine, large water tankage, etc. and yet be strong and safe enough to cross oceans, and with the capacity to carry sufficient stores for such a voyage. I was also influenced by Maurice Griffiths' shoal designs, particularly 'Lone Gull' and the article about that vessel's seaworthiness by the Yacht Research Society in the UK, and Griffiths' last design, Kylix, with his so-called 'loco cab'.

My five references were Douglas Phillips-Burt's book *Sailing Yacht Design*, Howard Chapelle's book, *Yacht Design and Planning*, a series of articles by Chuck Paine in Cruising World magazine on the parameters of yacht design, Lloyds' *Rules for the Construction of Glassfibre Yachts* and the bible of fibreglass yacht building, *Fibreglass Boats* by Hugo Du Plessis. I had another small volume which had graphs of design parameters plotted for many production yachts.

I should add that I did engineering drawing at University and TAFE and studied mathematics at University (Simpson's Rule is as hard as it gets in the mathematics of yacht designing), so getting down to studying what goes into designing a yacht was not as fearful for me as it might seem.

In many ways, the design of a yacht is a sculpture and a piece of art. A yacht designer must have some artistic spatial ability, which is able to translate a two dimensional drawing into the three dimensional thing of beauty. But, as we all know, beauty is in the eye of the beholder and, whilst the designs of William Fife III, Nat Herreschoff, G.L. Watson and others are exquisite pieces of beauty, the compromises that come with form and function are needs which must modify the purity of the art. Like an author who writes and rewrites over and over (D.H. Lawrence was one such author), the yacht designer rubs out and redraws many times before deciding to leave well enough alone. I always wanted one of those wonderfully mysterious devices called a planimeter and used for measuring irregular areas, but couldn't justify the cost.

I still see my design as a mass of compromises of one thing against or offsetting another. To do it again would assuredly produce something entirely different.

The experience of sailing the Walker 27(E), as I named that version of my design, showed what I did correctly and what could have been better. Because I lent more towards cargo carrying and seaworthiness than racing, my design was heavy and too fat in the middle for its length making it quite slow in anything less than strong breezes. But it was *safe* and easy to handle in tougher conditions. It wasn't heavily ballasted because, I believed, the raised mid-ship section would provide massive buoyancy in any sort of knockdown and although I did no calculations to prove it, would give a much smaller range of inverted stability than most modern wide beam yachts of today.

Later articles and a book by Tony Marchaj about the 1979 Fastnet Race debacle tended to support my thesis. Fortunately, in my years of sailing the Walker 27(E) I never had to face survival conditions. David Lewis, who purchased it from me, wrote to me about surviving a severe storm off the top of New Zealand in which other boats sank. He described how well my design rode out the conditions.

The flat sections adopted in the hull design, as suggested by the Yacht Research Society, I believe contributed to reduced rolling of the hull and improved comfort in bad conditions. Of course, placement of the ballast is the major contributor to rolling resistance with higher ballast reducing rolling and low placed ballast (deep keels) making rolling very quick and sick making – another advantage of shoal draft.

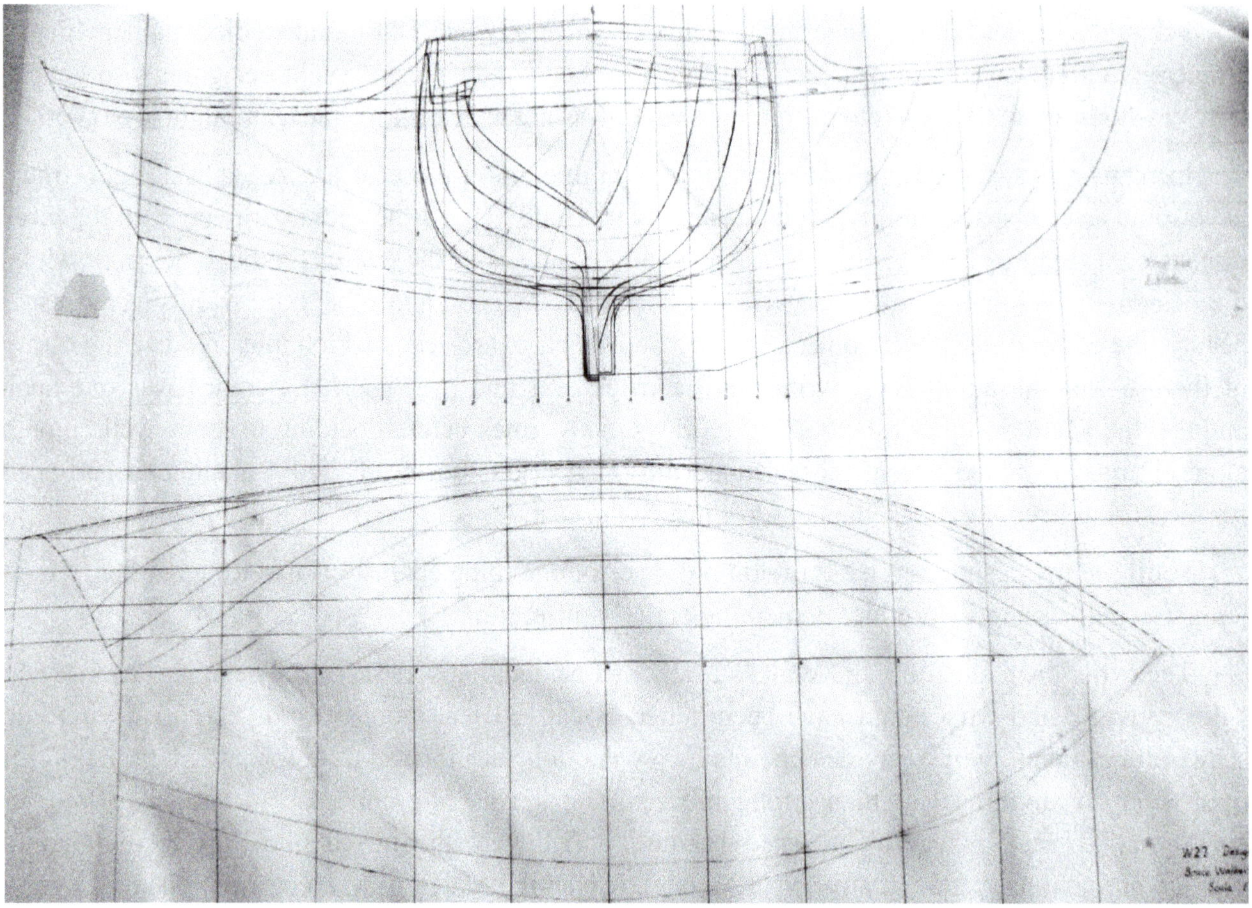

Lines plan – first attempt

Model from first lines plan

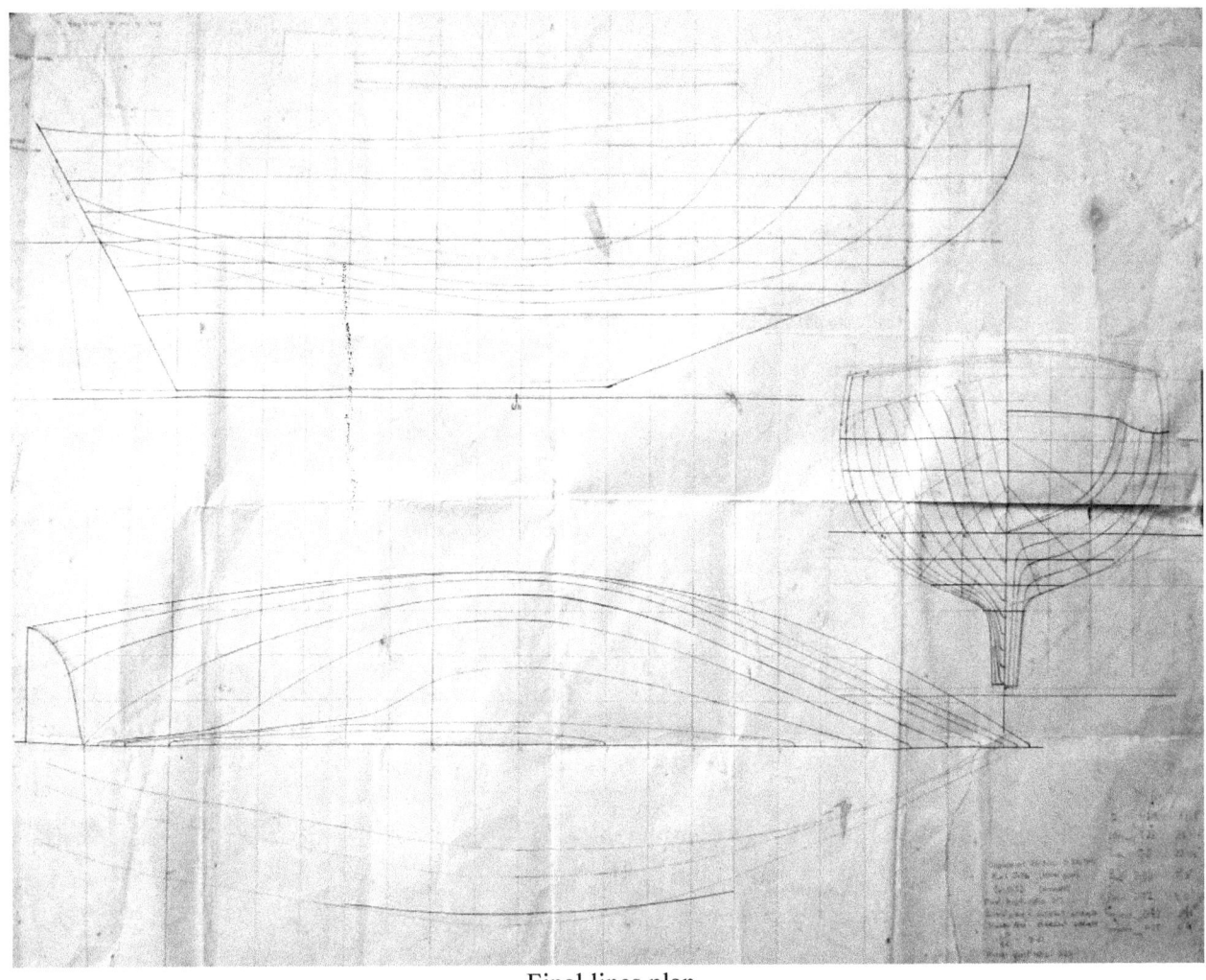

Final lines plan

Cynthia and I arrived in Bega with our new baby son, Douglas, and spent six years there. I worked on my design for the first two years and together we built a kit house out on ten acres some seventeen kilometres from Bega. Cynthia managed much of the home construction while I was at work, as well as looking after a very small child. At the end of two years, we moved out to our new house and built the big (boat building) shed during the next year. Late that year, I started cutting out and assembling frames for the yacht. The main glass fibre lay-up over the C-Flex, we did over Christmas, and the following year, I faired the hull as best I could. This is undoubtedly the worst part of glass fibre boat building and I resolved to never build a yacht in glass fibre again.During this time, two more children born in Bega came into the family. I spent evenings and weekends slowly labouring away. It was important not to neglect family fun and we spent many weekends with our friends, Jim and Helen Kelly and their children Sarah and Blake, picnicking at either of two nearby beaches, Picnic Point and Aragunnu. Both Beaches are located in the Mimosa Rocks National Park and at that time, were accessed through gates and rough dirt tracks. In the centre of Aragunnu Beach an old boiler from a shipwreck lay and, at Picnic Point, the bottom of the bay was covered with the rusting metal plates from another unnamed shipwreck.

C Flex Lay up showing scaffolding

I built a framework around my completed hull and, using chain blocks, attached to the walls of the shed, we slowly turned the hull over, first onto its side, then we dragged it across to the wall to make room to turn it upright.

The deck and fitting out began. There were many problems that had to be solved and, because of my isolation, I had no-one to turn to for advice; I made things up as I went along. In general, I don't think I got too much of it wrong. From a couple of planks of Huon Pine, I fashioned deckhead grab rails for the main cabin. I had the enormous bottom rudder pintle cast from gunmetal. It was held on by long stainless bolts and that was okay, but the nuts were of inferior stainless and eventually corroded away with electrolysis. However it held together. The jib was way too small and needed a bowsprit to improve balance.

Upturned hull with some moulds removed

Similarly, the rudder was too large and needed a fair chunk cut off it to reduce tiller load. A longer laminated tiller also helped. A few years later, I fitted an even longer bowsprit to give better balance and make the vessel much more gentle for self-steering.

The ballast was internal and, in the long keel, I made a series of glassed-in plywood webs to hold it together. I had cast a large lump of lead of approximately 1000lbs to drop into the largest central space in the keel. The rest of the ballast was in smaller ingots of around 20kgs.

On launching day, the large lump of lead was craned in, only to jam before it was fully in place. No amount of levering and attempts to re-position it by the crane could shift it. Sticking out like it did, I was unable to screw down the cabin sole. Later I spent weeks with a hammer and cold chisel cutting about three centimetres off the top. When I had finally finished all that effort, the lump suddenly just slipped into place. I was finally able to cement in all the ballast.

I bought a CMC 190C 10hp diesel engine, made in China, from the importer in Croydon Park – curiously, a Norwegian fellow called "Aussie" Flores.

The hull faring is complete. Three-year-old Douglas in the foreground

My visits to his premises were an education in themselves. The yard there was incredibly cluttered and it was only on my third visit was I able to discern a 50 foot steel yacht amongst the clutter. The engine I selected was an enormous 250kg single cylinder thing of cast iron. It came with every spare possible including piston and cylinder liner and a mass of tools for every sort of job.

This was a marinised version of an industrial engine which could be used for pumps, walking tractors and anything else you could think of. It had an evaporative cooling system that used a big hopper over the horizontal cylinder into which the operator poured buckets of water which boiled off as the engine ran.

The deck is painted

Keeping an eye on the water level was clearly important. I organised a one inch diameter copper pipe around six feet long as an external keel cooler. With some modifications this eventually worked quite well but there were other problems with this engine. The alternator on the engine was seriously pathetic. The main problem was that a one-third horsepower starter motor was simply not powerful enough to start the engine. A couple of clever marine electricians wired in a switch and solenoid arrangement, whereby when the starter button was pressed, 24 volts were fed to the starter motor. This worked quite well except on the occasion when we forgot the switch and an electrical fire started in the engine bay. These things always happen at the worst possible time like, when we were experiencing very strong winds, half way to Lord Howe Island on our first voyage there. Fortunately I was able to replace all the burnt out wiring and, provided one remembered to flick the switch, all worked as it should.

Aussie Flores persuaded me to trade up to a better version of the CMC Diesel, which I did with very little cash changeover. I forget how we did the engine swap, but this engine proved to have other problems.

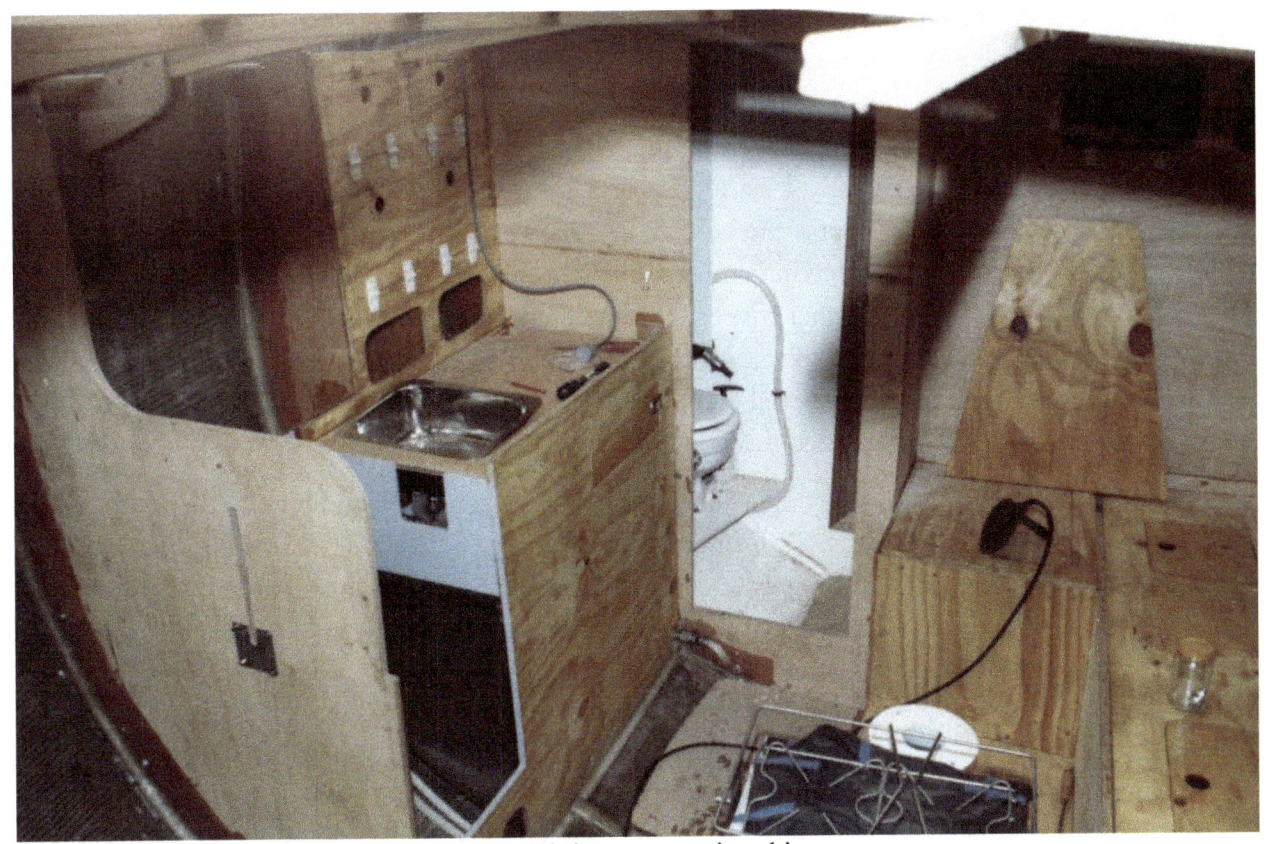
Fitting out – main cabin

Bruce fitting out main cabin (photo: Jim Kelly)

On the second engine, the alternator charged the batteries and, at two hp, the starter motor turned over the engine easily. However, the cooling system did away with my keel cooler and had a closed condenser system which required air to be pumped through a radiator-like device where the cooling water in the engine condensed. This required a continuous fan belt, as the drive lies between the engine and gearbox. Eventually I started using a segmented belt (similar to a Brammer Belt) sourced from Blackwoods. Of course the belts didn't last very long and always needed replacing at the most inopportune times. Not having conventional cooling required a dry exhaust. I had initially fitted a dry exhaust running through a copper, later stainless steel, 'French Head' emerging from the cabin roof. Later on, because of exhaust gases in our faces in the cockpit, I modified the exhaust pipe to pass through the transom. A tall stainless loop inside the cabin would, I hoped, prevent a wave rushing up the open exhaust and drowning the engine.

The other problem was that the engine and gearbox were separate and between them was a cush drive consisting of rubber blocks. Unfortunately, the power of the engine (10hp @ 1800 rpm) chewed out the rubber blocks very easily and it was a real pain to replace them. I fitted a PSS Shaft Seal from Porters and had no issues with leaking stern glands and the like. These seals work brilliantly and I later fitted one to *Revolution*.

Preparations for Cruising

Greg Coonan had been experimenting with a sheet-to-tiller system of self-steering. Self-steering was still available, even in extreme weather conditions, by the use of a storm jib set on an inner forestay. It worked as a steering sail when the other sails were reefed right down or wholly taken down. By using a series of shock cords, we provided the countering force on the tiller to balance the pull exerted by the steering sail. Surgical rubber was recommended, but I found shock cord in two thicknesses purchased from Whitworths quite satisfactory. To save having to buy a trysail, we had a very deep third row of reefing points sewn into the mainsail. The main was of a quite heavy Dacron, which I had cut down from an Adams 10 main. The jib that I specified was made in Hong Kong of tanned Dacron, and was set on a roller furler made by Bruce Sherwood at Sparcraft. It was intentionally high cut like a Yankee sail. I discovered on the drawing board that with a high cut sail, you don't have to adjust the position of the sheet car to any significant extent to obtain correct sail shape when the sail is progressively rolled in. I used Maxwell main sheet winches. By using a block with a becket on the sheet car and fitting small turning blocks to the sail clew, I could halve the load on the sheet at the only cost of having lots of jib sheet to pull in. I used mast-located winches to deal with the halyards and a small winch on the boom took care of the outhaul and slab-reefing.

My anchor of choice was a Bruce as it had no moving parts to skin one's knuckles – a problem I had found with Danforth types. The Bruce didn't work well with weedy bottoms and once, when anchored in Maitland Bay, it picked up a big round basketball sized lump of something or other which neatly filled the space between flukes and shaft. All chain rodes are considered best for anchoring anywhere near coral. I always carried at least three anchors and complete gear for them. We snagged our anchor twice and, to retrieve it, I used a loop of chain on a long line specifically made for the purpose.

Boats can be real money pits if you are not careful. In those days before GPS and when Satnav systems were very expensive, mastery of a sextant was essential. Although I had an English Ebbco plastic sextant, I found the US made Davis plastic job much easier to use and it served all my astro-navigation needs until GPS units became more widely available. To complete my instrumentation, I installed a good gimballed steering compass, a Walker Trailing Log with spares (I really don't think fish bite off impellers – the line wears out where it emerges from the bob weight or from the impeller, and breaks), and an inexpensive Radio Direction Finder. I also bought as many charts as I could afford.

For radio communication, I fitted a Wagner HF set with, I think, 10 crystals including a couple of pairs of duplex ones for Radphone. I joined Penta Comstat so that I could maintain some contact with Australia. On our Pacific Cruise, Greg Coonan and I used 27 meg radios to communicate with each other when in range. I did not have a VHF set which, on reflection, was a mistake. We carried a life raft in a valise below decks and an EPIRB in a grab bag with other sundry items like flares and reflectors.

I regard it as essential to be able to get a dinghy over the side in an emergency and the only answer is a hard dinghy unless you have an inflatable in davits or on the deck. Just imagine you've run aground on a falling tide and have to get an anchor out to windward to have any hope of getting yourself off. That is not the time to be thinking about inflating your dinghy. This scenario happened to us once in Port Stephens and I was glad of the hard dinghy. I'd made my seven-foot plywood pram dinghy some years previously and with a 2hp Suzuki on the stern it provided shore access transport for us all. It was also sufficient, when tied on the quarter, to move the mother vessel in still water – even 11 ton *Revolution*. A sculling notch in the middle of the stern of the dinghy could be used for propulsion if only one oar was available. Sculling is a skill worth learning and practising.

These days, old age has caught up somewhat and most of my sailing is in contesting the Summer Twilight Series at Drummoyne Sailing Club. We sailed *Top Knot* (a Top Hat 25) for a number of years after selling *Revolution* but Cynthia found it just too small. Although I made many improvements to *Waituri* over the years of ownership, I really wanted something a little faster and more competitive, so I bought *Mako* a Bonbridge 27. We have a new generation coming on and I'm keen to see how my little granddaughters take to sailing in the next few years.

Aragunnu's First Cruise

In 1976, Cynthia and I had owned our Southerly 23 for a couple of years and I resolved to move up to a larger boat. There was nothing available on the market that sufficiently caught my interest and a scheme to build a bigger boat had fallen through, so we made a decision late that year to design and build a yacht ourselves.

One has to earn a living and job pressures intervened. We found ourselves transferred, with our new-born son, to Bega on the far south coast of New South Wales. We spent the years 1977 and 1978 finding and buying a ten acre farmlet and building a house on it. At night, I proceeded with the yacht design. Midway through 1979, down from our house, I erected a 30 X 20 shed with a 12 foot ceiling. Lofting and male mould construction followed. Nearly two tons of kiln dried radiata pine went into this. In January 1980, Cynthia, pregnant with our second child, and I commenced the lay-up. By December, it was ready for turning over. Throughout 1981 and 1982, we added the furniture, the motor and the deck.

The construction moved along in remarkable isolation. No one I knew in the area was boat building. All my knowledge came from my extensive library.

After six years working in Bega, we were ready to make the move back up to Sydney. Both of us had lost a parent during this time, so getting back was more important than before. Cynthia gave birth to a third child, Jane, in late 1981. In August, I applied for a transfer and by December 1st, we knew the move was on. It would be a rush as *Aragunnu* was far from complete, let alone ready to be launched.

Ahead lay six weeks of holidays beginning on the 17th with work at the new posting due to start on 1st February. Pages and pages of job lists were before me. We set the tentative launching date for 5th January. But of course everyone was having their Christmas break. The low loader driver said he'd do it during the middle of his holidays on the 10th. Sparcraft, who were making the mast, were on break too, but Bruce Sherwood, the proprietor, kindly agreed to do the work as soon as I was able to give them forestay and backstay measurements (once the mast was up). Too late I found that the mail order chandlers, Whitworths and BIAS, also closed over the Christmas New Year period. With a sailing departure date set very tentatively for January 24th, it looked like we might be leaving without sheet winches, lifelines and stanchions. My 35lb plough anchor had been loaned to a Top Hat-owning friend who had sailed to the Great Barrier Reef. There he had run aground, had his boat salvaged and repaired. I wasn't sure when my anchor might come back, if ever. My father purchased a second anchor, a 22lb Bruce, and brought it down by train and bus.

Even that had problems. The train broke down near Waterfall and he had to carry the anchor plus his bag some distance up and down stairs. He was 73 years old.

My sailing cousin, Don Flecknoe, was rushing around Sydney trying to organise some second-hand sails based on my estimated luff measurements.

Launching day was almost upon us. The plough anchor arrived in the afternoon and at 6:30pm, Cynthia and I started winching the hull and cradle out of the shed and onto the landing to give the crane access to lift it onto the truck.

Our shed gives birth, December 1982

The next morning we had no time to think. The crane arrived an hour early while we were still in bed. The children dressed in seconds and yelling, raced outside. The low loader came shortly afterwards. The boat was lifted, the cradle transferred to the low loader, and then the workers lowered the boat back into its cradle. Ropes held all fast. The crane and low loader left in convoy for the fourteen mile dirt road trip to Bermagui for keel wetting.

Naturally, our friends who were coming to help hadn't arrived. With little appetite, we had breakfast and waited, knowing that the trucks would take it slowly.

Launching day, Bermagui December 1982 (Photo: Jim Kelly)

Wetting the keel (Photo: Jim Kelly)

Craning into Bermagui harbour began at 0915 hours. We expected the spectator crowd at 1030 so they missed the exciting bits. There were various minor traumas, such as the crane not having the proper slings, but by 1130 hours we had the mast standing, most of the lead ballast was in and our yacht was floating nicely on her designed lines. The spectator crowd attacked the chilled bottles of champagne

Alone on the foredeck, I poured twelve-year-old French Champagne onto the bow and christened the yacht *Aragunnu,* after a beach on the coast near our house.

Lowering 1000lb lump of lead (Photo: Jim Kelly)

On January 18th, the forestay, backstay, roller furler and sails arrived by truck from Sydney. During the afternoon a friend dropped by and we decided to do some motoring trials around the harbour. We made a quick decision to take the boat out into the ocean. Peter conned us through the narrow channel. There was some swell and the wind was from the east but at five knots or less. – Kadi, one of our visitor passengers, said she felt sick and asked that we take her back.

On Saturday morning with just two days to go, I picked up my cousin Don from Merimbula airport. He had made the one-hour flight down from Sydney in air-conditioned comfort so that he could spend two to four days returning in the usual cramped conditions of a small sailing yacht. That afternoon, we attempted a trial sail and again the wind from the east was less than five knots.

Sunday was to be our last opportunity for a sail and to sort out any bugs. It dawned hot and hazy with no wind and no swell. Jim Kelly, the third crewmember for the voyage to Sydney, was coming for his first sail. We slatted around in the bight north of Bermagui for a few hours and called it a day. We still hadn't had a proper sail and we really had to leave the next day.

Kingsley Press, the fourth crewmember and most experienced offshore sailor, arrived. A couple of years before, he and I had crewed to Lord Howe Island and back on the Top Hat, *Topaze*, mentioned earlier. I knew he was the right sort to have aboard especially if the going got tough. Because of his business commitments, he stepped aboard having not seen *Aragunnu* since it was in the shed, unpainted. These three fellows were showing remarkable faith, confidence and trust in my untried design and construction.

Almost everything was working out despite a pushpit arriving instead of a pulpit. We had no stanchions or lifelines but I had installed U-bolts and jackstays along each side deck for harness connections. Monday came with overcast skies and the hoped for southerly change. Now our luck was holding.

The southerly filled the sails and we set a course to pass the shoals south of Montague Island. Visibility was bad and we couldn't see the island although only ten miles off. I badly needed a whisker pole to hold the jib out.

We changed to a more northerly course three miles east of Montague Island and, by dusk, could make out the distinctive shapes of the Tollgates off Bateman's Bay. We had altered course to pick up the Brush Island light followed by the Warden Head Light near Ulladulla. During Don's 0330 to 0530 watch, a brilliantly lit fishing boat came close to investigate.

We altered course to clear Jervis Bay, which protrudes from the general line of the coast. In the dawn light we could see the high ground south of Jervis Bay.

The wind deserted us during the day so we started the motor. Somehow the water had escaped from the cooling system, causing the motor to boil, run dry and stop. It was our first crisis. But had it seized? With some trepidation I decompressed and tried the starting handle. Fortunately it turned easily.

Twenty-eight hours had passed since leaving and we were halfway, but further use of the motor seemed doubtful. Through the afternoon we crept past Jervis Bay. The south-running current moves close to the coast here, so we were pushing against that as well. A Naval Patrol vessel passed a few hundred yards across our bow and another passed astern, both heading for the Naval Base in the bay.

The wind remained light and variable with progress depressingly slow. We set our course straight across Shoalhaven Bight. By late afternoon, the lights of Gerringong at the northern end of the bight were in view. The wind settled to about five knots from the north-east with waves from the same direction on a low swell. Our sail area was just too small to make reasonable progress against a combination of wind, waves and current. For nearly twelve hours we tacked back and forth to gain five miles of coastline. With the dawn, Kiama was clearly visible.

A unanimous vote from the crew directed me to the engine and to see if anything could be done. The rubber impellor was in tiny pieces. I re-routed the hoses to by-pass the leaking header tank. I removed the cover on the top of the engine hopper, so that cool water could be poured directly onto the cylinder. That is the way these Chinese Dong Feng diesels are cooled when used in their various agricultural roles in China. We re-started the motor and after two hours, it was hot but not boiling.

The north-easterly continued to freshen during the day. We'd taken a long tack offshore to clear Bass Point then we began the long tack back inshore towards the smoking steelworks at Port Kembla. The wind continued to rise and we took a second reef in the mainsail and a few rolls of the jib. It didn't seem that long since we'd been cursing our lack of canvas.

As we came further inshore, the steepness of the waves increased. Almost among the five rocky islets off Port Kembla, Jim and Kingsley struggled to tack us. The wave motion kept pushing the bow around and we kept losing momentum. Finally on the third or fourth try, with rocks only 150 yards ahead and a backed jib, we slowly wore around to the other tack onto a safer course taking us due east. We held this course for six hours but were only making two or three knots. Finally the wind began to die and we were able to bring ourselves around to a course with a lot more northing in it.

By midnight we could see the powerful sodium street lights at the top of the escarpment above Bulli Pass, north of Wollongong. The coastline from there is National park and there are no lights. I felt it prudent to head off shore again. Poor visibility had prevented me from obtaining a fix with the hand-bearing compass so we could only guess at how far offshore we were.

When I took the helm from Jim at 0130 a south easterly had sprung up. Jim had enjoyed a brisk northwesterly for most of his two hours. Our course was maintained through my watch and Don's which followed. The wind backed to the south and picked up quite considerably. We called Kingsley and together, dropped the mainsail altogether. The weight in the tiller ceased moving Don's light frame across the cockpit.

By dawn, the wind was really blowing hard. The sky was grey and overcast with whitecaps on waves everywhere. Kingsley, on watch since 0530, really prefers this sort of weather. We began to close the coast.

By 0900, we could make out the grey shapes of Kurnell Oil Refinery on the southern shores of Botany Bay. The swells seemed enormous. A ship steaming south directly into it had about a quarter of its length out of the water as it crested each swell.

We passed through Sydney Heads at 1130 hours. It was January 27th.

The voyage showed up many faults in the various systems. Later, I modified the engine cooling and it gave no further problems. The rudder was too much the 'barn door' and I lopped off a big piece and I increased the sail area dramatically with the addition of a bowsprit. I found a number of

U-bolts attaching the stays to the deck to be inferior and replaced them. But the basic hull and construction proved sound and subsequent voyages have shown her to be a tough little yacht. Although slow, perhaps her best feature is her very gentle motion, being at home on the ocean wave and giving her crew confidence.

Aragunnu in Sydney Harbour – no bowsprit yet

Mainsheet cover Feb 1986

    I thought I was enjoying myself until someone pointed to our catalogue of disasters. First up, I strained my back pulling up the anchor, resulting in agony for some days. A kindly crewmember from one of our other Club yachts gave me an excellent massage (closely watched by Cynthia). Secondly, our four year old daughter, Jane, was bitten on the stomach by a horse, which I would have thought was not an accident normally associated with yacht cruising. Later the same day, New Year's Eve, she put a horrid cut in her wrist. The folk from Gwandalan Aquatic Club, where we were to have our New Year's Eve party, generously provided transport to a doctor for four stitches. Fortunately there were no severed tendons and no tears from a brave child. Thirdly, in a quiet raft-up with *Nanook,* wash from a passing powerboat resulted in a broken cleat, smashed gunwale and fairlead.

Next, we ran aground on Sand Point near Corlette in Port Stephens. That story is told elsewhere. Fortunately the whole incident resulted in no harm being done and cemented my subsequent friendship with David and Margaret from *Sunflower*.

Later, back at Lake Macquarie, a stern line from *Aragunnu* to R.M.Y.C wharf at Toronto chafed through allowing *Aragunnu* to swing into an H28 called *Believe Me* whose owner had just spent $600 having the gunwales refurbished and varnished. *Aragunnu* did a job on that. I thought the poor old bugger was going to have a heart attack. He didn't say much. The bill was $300. Then, on the day we left, Cynthia, not to be outdone by me, pulled muscles in her back while struggling with a dinghy half-filled with rainwater.

The cruise over, back home we discovered a blocked sink, a dripping tap, flooded kitchen, buckled lino, warped cupboard doors and a ruined electric frypan. Then a day or two later, just to round off everything, our house was broken into. The thief took our video player and various other stuff.

It was hardly a holiday. I was glad to get back to work.

To the South Pacific

Sixty years ago, setting out on a voyage such as we did in a vessel the size of *Aragunnu* with a wife and three small children, I would have been regarded by most people as, at best, probably certifiable. Thirty years ago I would have been labeled irresponsible. But in the eighties, well-wishers inquired if there was room for one more. They told me that I was very brave and to have a good time. Times change. By contrast, my 76 year old father, always one to offer encouragement, said, "Well son, I don't suppose I'll see you again."

Thanks Dad for the thumbs up, I thought.

Long voyages in small boats are becoming commonplace. I do not consider myself brave. In a sense, one's voyage through life is about playing the odds, covering the bets and being prepared as best you can. *Aragunnu* as she was before we went to the South Pacific

Before I list my toll of unforeseen disasters guaranteed to turn anyone off ocean voyaging forever, allow me to diverge slightly.

The author of a recent boating magazine article suggested that there is no such thing as bad luck. He wrote that each time you do maintenance on your boat, inspect or check equipment or replace worn parts, you are storing credits in the bank. Voyagers with lots of credit points, such as the Hiscocks, rarely experience so called bad luck. Similarly, Murphy's Law would have it that the part you didn't check would be the one that failed.

Aragunnu as she was when we left for the South Pacific

Our shakedown cruise had been in the August-September school holidays in 1985. In company with our friends, the Coonans aboard *Nanook*, we set out for Lord Howe Island, us from Sydney Harbour and the Coonans from Broken Bay. Curiously we met them midway over. Cynthia and I took our oldest son, Douglas, and a friend, Bob McNamara. Our younger children stayed with their grandmother.

Douglas, aged eight years, started to keep a log of the voyage. Doug's writing is as he wrote it, including spelling errors:

First Night –arrived at the boat round nine. We left mooring at eleven thirty. We motored to the heads. I thought it was boring. I also felt tied sitting out in the cockpit. We put the sails up as we went along. I went to bed round Lady Jane's beach

First Day Got up at six. Talked to Dad to nine then through up. After that stayed in bed. Got up at noon and through up again. Bob vomited next. Had nothing the hole day till six. I had scorched peanuts then went to sleep.

Day Two.

The log ends here, perhaps Douglas tired of recording all his vomiting.

We had some big seas on the way over with waves I estimated as higher than our spreaders but, fortunately, not breaking. An electrical problem that I inadvertently caused produced a fire in the engine bay. I put it out with a messy dry powder fire extinguisher. Sitting on the exposed engine, I re-wired the burnt out electrics. As always seems to be the case, it was the middle of the night and the seas were very rough. Cynthia came below after steering for three hours and Bob took over. I was asleep. After a while, Cynthia asked Bob if he was enjoying it out there. He told her he would rather be in the cabin and she told him she would rather be in the cockpit, so she went out again and steered until dawn. Breaking waves were coming aboard and she remembers constantly pulling the jib sheets out of the two inch bore cockpit drains as water slopped into the foot-well.

We spent three days aboard in the lagoon during a storm, held beam-on to the wind by the current in the lagoon and thus well-heeled over. The storm passed but the seas remained big outside the reef. With just a few days of holidays left and the need to get back to work, we made the decision to leave the island. To get out of the lagoon, we had to pass out through the North Passage which is a narrow opening in the coral. Looked at it from the shore, it didn't seem too bad so we decided to go for it. *Nanook* went first and hit a set of larger breaking waves as they went through. Similarly *Aragunnu* faced breaking waves of about ten feet in height.

I can truthfully say it was the most frightening experience I have ever had in my years of sailing. We were harnessed on and Douglas, in his lifejacket, carried an open knife to cut himself free and swim for shore if the unthinkable happened.

Nanook and *Aragunnu* at Lord Howe Island 1985

Out in the open water the sea settled and, after that day, we had a very pleasant sail back to Sydney arriving in good time to get back to work. I felt that we had well and truly been blooded.

For 1986, I thought I had been thorough in checking things and eliminating systems likely to fail, yet virtually everything that went wrong fell into the categories of lack of maintenance or failure to replace after "x" years of service. The man who can in all honesty say, "Look at that rigging, it's in perfect condition. I haven't had to touch it in ten years probably shouldn't go voyaging. Jon Sanders replaced all the rigging on *Perie Banou* with rigging double the size, before leaving on his double circumnavigation. I should have done similarly. There's no place for broken shrouds in the middle of the ocean.

I had left that weeping port water tank. It had been too difficult to remove or attend to. Rough seas and sloshing water turned the leak from a trickle into a torrent and the best part of forty three gallons of precious water disappeared into the bilge. Fortunately, being of a belts and braces mentality, it was less than half our total capacity. The Morse cable on the engine throttle linkage was next. When did I last grease the cable? Well, I haven't because it always works okay. There's no excuse for flat batteries that are so easy to check regularly with the hydrometer. Wisely, I had a fully charged spare for the radio and the like, but the main batteries were so flat they looked like they might not recover. How often does one go about the deck, caulking gun handy and throw buckets of water against various deck fittings? Most modern sealants do their job incredibly well while they're new, but it doesn't take long before they harden, letting water in. There's nothing like some rough seas to find all your deck leaks. Old style sealants like butyl mastic never harden and may be the best to use.

My new storm jib didn't last the first storm. Now I know why they recommended a bolt-rope, sewn all round. I suppose that in dealing with riggers, spar makers and sailmakers you should insist on getting what you want and not allow them to talk you into some compromise.

An old rule for the breaking strain of a cap shroud was that it should be equal to the displacement of the vessel. I suspect you won't find too many yachts rigged to this specification.

Leaving on the 7th July 1986, we sailed briskly on course for some hours until the inevitable headwinds set in. We had been becalmed for six hours with Port Stephens just over the horizon and the light looms of Sydney and Newcastle, away in the southwest. July would appear to be the windiest month, a view supported by the pilot charts.

After the calm, *Aragunnu* rolled off the miles covering mostly around 120 miles with a record day, for us, of 144 miles and this, generally, with one or two reefs in the mainsail and a few rolls in the jib.

Unfortunately these terrific mileages didn't translate into useful progress in the direction we wanted to go. Days and days of northerly and northeasterly winds rarely below 15 knots pushed us just off the bottom of my chart and I found myself plotting our position in the margin but finally a south-westerly arrived, allowing us to run northwards.

After a week, we were only a couple of hundred miles past Lord Howe Island. Daily positions on the chart looked like we were making an inspection tour of the Tasman Sea and not heading anywhere in particular. Finally with Norfolk Island in view some ten or so miles distant, we had day after day of south-easterly.

It seemed as if we had reached the southern limit of the trade winds so off we plunged again with reefed sails in an east-nor'-east direction. About this time, I discovered the port aft lower shroud with seven strands of wire broken (in 1 by 19 SS wire), fortunately on the leeward side.

Everyone on board had settled into the daily routines. Seasickness pills were no longer necessary. The boys were doing their homework, set by their teacher mother, Cynthia, and had discovered the joys of reading books. Cynthia and I were working through our store of paperbacks, sometimes one a day. Lego, Plasticine, coloured pencils, crayons and paper occupied the children when they weren't eating or sleeping. The usual boisterous behaviour of the children was toned down.

The sighting of Norfolk Island confirmed my navigational accuracy from taking sextant sights mid-morning and mid-afternoon. I had spent a sleepless night mulling over what to do with the broken stay. I had swapped the forward and aft lowers as there seemed to be more load on the aft lowers but that was really only a temporary solution. My sleepless night produced two possible options. Cynthia suggested looping rope over the mast tang and taking it to the chain plate. I worked out a system of tensioning the line so it was not a whole lot less tensioned than the stay. Pre-stretched terylene line has a high breaking strain even allowing for the losses due to the system of knots in it.

Then I put my mind to the broken throttle cable. I worked out a solution once the damaged bit had been lopped off. We motored past Norfolk Island as I saw no point in stopping. It was calm and, after some time, I was relieved to see that the batteries were starting to recover.

I dread climbing the mast even in Five Dock Bay, so my feelings about going up the mast, on a rocking boat in the open ocean with ten to fifteen knots of wind, can only be described by my extremely dry mouth and very hot sweating palms. I needed to go only to the spreaders, about seventeen feet, but it had to be done. Not long after my ride in the bosun's chair, which left me with bruises and pinched skin on my inner thighs from banging on the mast, we had a blow of around 30 or 40 knots from the north-west lasting 24 hours and putting plenty of strain on the port lowers. Everything held and we started to feel confident in our makeshift repairs. The wind finally subsided and moved around to the south-west and we had magnificent sailing conditions with Aragunnu rolling off the miles. We had been at sea for sixteen days, and had our first radio contact with our friends, the Coonans, aboard *Nanook*.

The original plan was to meet them in Fiji after their stopover in Tonga. They had left seven weeks before us and had visited Lord Howe, Raoul Island in the Kermadecs, then sailed to Tongatapu and were sailing through the Ha'pai Group towards Vav'u the northernmost group of Tongan Islands. They suggested we join them in Tonga and that they would wait for us there. So we decided to change our destination to Neiafu, the capital of Vava'u. This meant a few extra days and I was a little concerned about our water supplies. We normally have a fairly low salt diet but cAnnd food is loaded with it so we were drinking more fluids. However, there was no need for water rationing.

We were becalmed again on the nineteenth day, so ran the engine. After four hours the batteries had improved considerably. I was still loathe to use the navigation lights as they seemed such a heavy drain and I was using only a tricolour masthead light. I was relying on other ships picking up the Firdell Blipper Radar Reflector to spot us, more than lights. My daily skeds with Penta Comstat reporting our position were short and I didn't think used much battery.

The third time we were becalmed the third gale followed. By dark, according to my hand held anemometer, the wind had risen to around forty knots. We decided to run under storm jib alone. My repairs were holding. The seas were rough and the teeming rain felt like needles on any exposed skin, reminding me of those awful showers in the change rooms at Coogee Aquarium when I was a child. We couldn't look to windward because of the rain and spray and the occasional wave breaking over us.

The cabin in a storm is a wonderful place. It feels so secure and far from the anger and violence with the door shut. The need to brace oneself and the swaying tea towels and kero lamp are the only signs of what's happening outside. Even the noise seems less frightening. There is the fear of being rolled when the big waves smash over us and the pounding of the waves is disconcerting. However I know I made our boat as strong as I could and we all feel safe and secure, playing music cassettes loudly to drown out some of the noise. We sang along, knowing all the words of every song by now.

Cynthia announced that she wouldn't be celebrating her birthday, due in three days, until we had anchored.

The progress seemed slower with the daily dots on the chart becoming closer together. I couldn't help feeling a bit impatient – impatient to be through the reefs and hazards ahead and safely anchored. I guess all voyagers have these sorts of feelings as a landfall approaches. I read that, once land is in sight, many, feel a reluctance to enter port, perhaps regretting the end of the voyage. We weren't like that.

Then we sighted Ata, the southernmost island of the Tongan Kingdom. We had only a couple of hundred miles to go with the wind a steady 15 to 20 knots from the southwest. The next day we were sailing past the distinctive islands of Tofua and Kao. Both are high with Kao to the north an almost perfect cone shape, and Tofua a truncated cone with a central lagoon.

I later realised we had sailed over almost the exact spot on the earth's surface where the mutiny on the Bounty had taken place 197 years earlier (ten miles east of Tofua). Bligh was a bit of an unfortunate chap. Prior to the publication of the book by Charles Norhof and James Norman Hall, *The Mutiny on the Bounty,* Bligh had been regarded as not quite the evil tyrannical martinet the book made him out to be.

Later court evidence indicated that Bligh was subject to intense irrational anger outbursts, often directed at Christian, but he was otherwise normal. Fletcher Christian, as portrayed in three different cinematic films by Errol Flyn, Clark Gable and Mel Gibson, was the dashing handsome hero who took his lovelorn companions back to their loved ones in Tahiti, and not the leader of a rabble of over-sexed impressed men who had only one thing on their minds. Poor old unlucky Bligh faced a second rebellion in his life when confronted by booze-mad marines in 1805. Sex-crazed sailors and booze-crazed soldiers – sex and alcohol does it every time.

Interestingly, one of Cynthia's father's best friends once owned Bligh's sextant. Unfortunately it was stolen.

Our last day had some disappointments. At dawn we were heading towards an island which we thought might be Vava'u, but turned out to be Late Island. We then realised we had a nearly thirty mile beat to windward and clearing customs that day wouldn't be possible.

Almost suddenly it was over. There we were with eleven miles to go to the Vava'u Group, with *Nanook,* who had sailed out to meet us. They were alongside, everyone, Greg, Ann, Paul, Joanne and Leigha waving and shouting and taking photos.

After twenty-six days at sea, we anchored in a superb little bay and watched our anchor drop 30 feet to the bottom and the chain flake out along the sand. The water was clearer and bluer than I'd ever seen before.

Seeing the anchor touch bottom and feeling the cool water wash over our bodies and the sand between our toes more than made up for the morning.

Aragunnu closes Vav'u, Tonga (Photo: Greg Coonan)

Aragunnu in the Kingdom of Tonga

We spent our first night in Tonga anchored quietly near *Nanook*. The next morning, we motored some miles to Neiafu, the capital of Vava'U, to clear customs and officially enter Tonga. We seemed to be heading up a long fiord with sides a hundred or more feet high. It reminded me a little of the Hawkesbury except that the sides were a little lower and covered with palm trees. The water was an astonishing shade of blue. Some of the small islands are cut away at the water's edge and resemble mushrooms.

We were ordered to tie to the wharf and three men came aboard: a Customs officer who was interested in whether we carried alcohol or firearms. It seems that most American yachts carry firearms hidden aboard, or at least some impressive archery. We answered "no" to the firearms question and showed the officer a ruptured wine cask in the bilge. An agriculture officer was interested in the fruit and vegetables on board; and a policeman had forms for us to fill out for immigration. We were granted a visa for one month and we were told to write a letter to the Postmaster asking permission to cruise the islands, naming which islands we intended to visit and when. The Postmaster was very gracious, made notes on our letter, stamped and filed it.

Being a Friday, Neiafu was chock-a-block with people. They come from their villages in long, low row boats loaded down by large Tongan folk, some with umbrellas, and goods to sell at the markets. These boats are clinker or carvel and similar to surfboats, mostly with powered by a 9hp Yamaha outboard on the stern. Some years ago I sold a 5hp British Seagull to a missionary who was taking it to Tonga but on our visit, I saw only Yamahas. The day is spent in town and at the end of the day the older children are collected from high school and taken home. Monday is a repeat performance in the reverse order.

You can really feel you are in a foreign country. The town streets, whilst tarred, are dusty and narrow with a kind of Wild West appearance. There are a lot of shops, all of weatherboard with corrugated iron rooves. The insides have floors of swept concrete and behind the all-round counter are shelves stacked with goods to sell. A girl looks after about four feet of counter and laboriously writes every item on your receipt. Many folk are in the shop and outside socialising and making purchases. The sights and smells are so unfamiliar to our Australian senses. All the stores are the same, selling exactly the same range of products. We thought of the cold weather Sydney was experiencing and wiped the perspiration from our eyes. Tucked away in amongst the islands with no sea breezes, Neiafu seemed oppressive and sweltering.

Tongans are big people. The men are handsome and the girls are attractive although strong and robust looking. I can understand why they were some of the supreme warriors of the South Seas, often acting as mercenaries for their neighbours. I certainly wouldn't want to face them on a football field, which is a popular sport here.

Whilst Neiafu and Vav'u have been discovered by tourists, there aren't many and it is still relatively unspoiled. I saw only one souvenir shop, but there is a big industry in wood carving, baskets, shell work, necklaces and jewelry. Prices are low, yet I was told one hundred percent more expensive than just a few years ago. Bargaining is the order of the day and prices can be reduced by 20%. The Coonans showed their expertise with Ann being a particularly tough buyer.

If you're prepared to eat the local food you could survive here for years on next to nothing. A great basket of paw paws costs one dollar, a basket of coconuts is one dollar, a big branch of bananas is two dollars. Fish is also correspondingly cheap. The stuff on the shelves is about double the price of that in supermarkets back in Sydney. Tongans regard pawpaw as pig food and there are a lot of pigs wandering around in the villages. Tongans love their pork but they are quietly amused when foreigners eat pawpaw as they know eating too much of it can have volcanic effects on the bowels. Custard apples here are huge, close to football size and nothing like the puny items found in Australia. They are delicious and sweet. Lying under trees we picked up pamplemousse. These are a citrus of almost pumpkin proportions. The skin is around an inch thick and the final peeled size perhaps a little larger than a grapefruit. The interior is dark pinkish and the flavour rather bland, not bitter like a grapefruit, but not as sweet as an orange.

A couple of times, while walking along a dusty road, we'd hear a quiet voice asking us if we wanted a drink. It would come from a young chap, way up near the top of a coconut palm. A few coconuts would be dropped to the ground and the young man would shimmy down. With a couple of flicks with his machete, he would prepare drinking coconuts for us, even to the extent of a bit of rolled leaf to function as a straw. These were superbly refreshing drinks, slightly effervescent. The inside of a drinking coconut does not have the white chewy stuff of mature coconuts, which they dry into copra, but a thick creamy substance which you can scrape off with your fingernail and enjoy.

There are many other yachts here, mostly U.S. or N.Z. flagged, with a smattering of Australians and Canadians. A charter fleet is based here of the typical Caribbean yacht, some 40 to 46 foot long with a Bimini top, Hibachi and so on. Having cruised up from Nuku'alofa, Greg and Ann seem to know most of the yachties already and we are swamped with introductions to thin, deeply tAnnd cruising folk with a wide variety of accents, all friendly and interested. Few boats have children and three children is very rare. The twenty six day passage direct from Sydney caused the raising of eyebrows and I felt we had done something unusual even in yacht cruising.

I knew I was settling into the cruising mode when faced with another job, I thought, "Why do it today, when there's always tomorrow." I did fashion a temporary aft lower stay out of quarter inch galvanised wire rope using wire rope grips of which I had a good supply. This lasted for the remainder of our trip.

We spent several days at Ano Beach on the island of Pangai Motu. About a dozen yachts were anchored here and Greg and Ann introduced us to a number of their crews. We were starting to remark that Greg's middle name was 'Arious'. One couple we met had lost their satellite navigation (called SatNav – no GPS in those days) and were rowing around the anchorage asking for someone to teach them how to navigate with a sextant. They had found Tonga only by sailing in a search pattern.

In the evening we decided to try out our Radphone service and make a phone call to Cynthia's mother in Sydney. I'd had Radphone crystals fitted to our Wagner HF Radio just before leaving. The call went through okay but for ten minutes we had Cynthia screaming into the microphone, "Mum, it's me, Cynthia!!" Followed by a voice saying, "Is that you Cynthia?" We gave up. On deck, Greg on *Nanook,* called across the dark water, "She probably would have heard you better if you'd just stood on deck and yelled."

Cruising lethargy was taking over and we were staying too long in some places. We walked and caught a bus into Neiafu. The two islands are connected by a causeway. On the walk we picked and ate wild mandarins growing beside the road. They probably belonged to someone but no-one was around. They were quite bitter but otherwise okay and juicy.

Even the water seemed warm but was considered by the Tongans, and those who arrived from Samoa or Tahiti, as too cold for swimming. It was hard to get some relief from the constant heat. Sweat poured off me. I guess my body was designed for a cooler European climate.

We motored to Taunga, which is the smallest inhabited island in the Vava'u Group. Our anchor hit the bottom in ten feet of water at one of those perfect picture postcard beaches, with a long curve of blinding white sand, overhung with swaying coconut palms and tropical greenery with crystal clear blue sparkling water. I imagined a film crew making a Coca Cola advertisement there. A steel double-ender flying a Swedish flag departed shortly after our arrival and we were joined by *Taurangi*, a William Aiken designed timber Ingrid, with Miguel, Annie and their two young daughters aboard. Miguel was regarded with some reverence by some, for having crewed with Bernard Moitessier – one of cruising's living legends.

Anchored further out were Kevin and Jill in a steel Adams 45 extended to 49', all the way from Brisbane. There was also a New Zealand couple in a superbly built aluminum Adams 12 named *Foreigner*. Unfortunately the wind started to strengthen from our most exposed direction and departure became necessary. We re-anchored in Port Maurelle, the safe bay where we had anchored on our first night and rafted up with *Nanook*. The wind outside freshened to gale force and the bay slowly filled with yachts waiting out the weather. We didn't know we'd spend a week there while wind warnings were reissued each day.

Aragunnu at anchor Port Maurelle

Here Greg introduced us to Brett and Trish, a New Zealand couple in *Shaula*, a 26 foot heavy displacement yacht close to completing a circumnavigation via the Cape of Good Hope and the Magellan Straits. We spent several evenings enjoying Brett's excellent storytelling. He showed a piece of his hull planking which had been pierced by a swordfish with the bit of the fish sword still in the wood. The winds and the kelp beds to be found in the Magellan Straits sounded fearsome and Greg resolved never to sail there. I thought the cooler climate might be nice.

We walked to the two villages on the island picking and eating wild mandarins on the way. A final party on the shore was attended by crews of the remaining boats. Most of the conversation was about the passage to Fiji and the lack of trade winds this year. For most, the cruising in Tonga was drawing to a close and Fiji beckoned.

We met Ian, cruising in a UK registered Ohlson 35 with his wife and baby son. He was slowly working his way home to Australia after an absence of fourteen years. He proved to be a true yachting vagabond, full of all the sharp information on how to do it on the cheap, what to trade, where to go and so on.

We teamed up with Liz and Lou on *Silver Cloud*, two years out of Dana Point, California, and slowly making their way west. They proved to be a great couple and the days of storytelling and card playing started to turn to weeks. Our three yachts visited Hunga, an island on the western side of the group, with a virtually land-locked lagoon accessible through a tiny narrow entrance less than a boat length wide. The islanders were having a film night. The projector was powered by a noisy generator and the films shown on an outdoor screen for everyone were *Ben Hur* and *The Ten Commandments*, it being Sunday, and the Tongans very religious. We were advised never to work on our boats on a Sunday, as the 'day of rest' is taken very literally. But, right on midnight, when it became Monday, on came *Rambo*. The children were enthralled but most of the little village children were asleep on their mother's laps. We passed up on *Rambo*.

I was starting to develop a picture of the sort of person who gives up their job, sells or lets their house and heads off on an indefinite cruise. I noticed something they all had in common. Of course I am aware that there will be exceptions but at that stage I hadn't met any. They have all been migrants. Liz and Lou had migrated to the USA from Canada, Jim and Eileen on *Zaidah* from the UK to NZ, another on a Westsail 32 from South Africa to Canada, Brett from South Africa to NZ and so on. Thinking about it, it would seem that people who have not established such firm roots in a country find it easier to leave, easier to break the ties of family, job and house than others. I imagine that the exceptions are people whose dream is very strong and who show persistence and determination to realise that dream. Having a great deal of willpower would be the essential requirement. Itinerant lifestyles, created by the type of employment, might also make breaking away easier.

In company with Liz and Lou on *Silver Cloud*, a Nelson 41, which we privately christened 'the sailing junkyard" due to the sheer amount of stuff they had on board, we motored around to an island which has a largely reef-bound anchorage.

Since that first burst of wind that kept us in Port Maurelle, the SE trade winds had arrived. We snorkeled over the coral and admired the brightly coloured fish. Greg had mentioned Kenutu as a destination. Actually, he nagged us about it incessantly. Kenutu lies on the fringing reefs on the far eastern side of the Vav'u Group. The passage required negotiating a dog-leg pass through coral reefs but was worth it and apologies were made to Greg. We congratulated him on his excellent choice.

Within minutes of our anchors touching the sandy bottom, we saw a New Zealand couple running frantically on the beach. In just knee deep water they had caught, by hand, the most extraordinary lobster any of us had ever seen. We took photos to remind ourselves and show others that we weren't exaggerating about just how large it was. It seemed a pity that such a beautiful creature would end up in a cooking pot. The cooking pot required would need to be huge.

On the adjoining island, Greg took us to see 'the cave'. This is a hole in the ground caused by some subterranean subsidence about fifty feet across and eighty or so feet down a slope to a pool. The water is quite cold and salty so it is likely fed from the sea and about the same level as the sea outside. It was a hot day so we enjoyed its refreshing chill in the gloomy light. We muddied ourselves somewhat, climbing back up the slope. On the beach were two Tongan fishermen. They seemed incongruous with their long trousers, shirts and jackets, a packet of tobacco protruding from a pocket, and their little outrigger canoe. They would spend all night fishing, come back with half a dozen fish, cook a couple on the beach, have a sleep for a few hours then go out again.

One of the main events on the Neiafu calendar is the Agricultural Show. We returned for it, knowing the King would be attending. Luckily on the way there, all ten of us were given a lift. The show is held in the grounds of a modern high school with each village mounting a display of their goods and products. Yams seemed to be the most common, but all other fruits and vegetables were represented. One stall was a tray about sixty feet long with all kinds of fish. It was rather smelly, too. A number of the shops had displays of their wares as well. About half the show comprised handicrafts: basketwork, tapa cloths, shell jewelry and brightly sewn bedspreads and pillow slips (one embroidered with "Kiss me quick") and so on. Judges busied themselves everywhere.

The King arrived at ten o'clock amid much fanfare and the ceremonial part began. The speeches in Tongan seemed interminable, however a check with my watch showed it about as long as a wedding (and equally tedious). The singing and dancing followed. The King made a tour in a mini-moke – he is very large – then handed out trophies and certificates to all the prizewinners of which there were many. Interestingly, one is not allowed to stand in the presence of the King. I suppose one's head must be below his. I remember his mother, Queen Salote, had cut quite a figure at the Melbourne Olympics endearing herself to Australians everywhere.

By twelve midday, everyone was packing up and going home. The rain poured down and we trudged back into town soaking wet.

The King looked older than his pictures on the banknotes and being of considerable size, he has difficulty moving around, using a chrome walking stick. He was educated at Newington College and Sydney University where he obtained his BA and LLB and was the first Tongan to graduate from University. Seeing the King and the Show was something of a highlight to our visit to Tonga. The singing, dancing and traditional costumes were superb and impressive.

One of the shops had an ice cream machine on the verandah. It was a bit of a lottery if it was working when you got there, and that the waiting crowd was not too long to exhaust the machine before it was your turn. That was fun.

The outside fresh bread cabinet was always alive with swarms of cockroaches. That kind of put us off eating the bread which otherwise looked quite good. The shops sell 'cabin bread', long a staple of seafarers. A tin of this is of about 4 gallon size and when opened is sealed with silver foil. The stuff is more biscuit than bread and very much like an Australian Sao biscuit, about the same size, but thicker and heavier. They last a long time and are good eating, spread with tinned butter and jam or peanut butter, or cheese and tomato, or anything really.

The next day, after frantic shopping, we cleared customs for Suva. The mass of images were still fresh. Our twenty seven days spent in Tonga had flown and suddenly it was over and time to move on. The reef strewn waters of Fiji lay ahead.

Aragunnu in Fiji

The passage to Suva from Vava'u is about four days sailing. Stretched in between Tonga and Fiji are a chain of Islands, the Lau Group. Foreigners are forbidden from going there. This was the most nerve-racking passage of our whole cruise. My navigation and the courses we were steering were not corresponding. On top of that, Cynthia had developed a severe earache and was not able to help as much as usual. We had to thread our way between the islands. There were some navigation lights to guide us during the night but I didn't see any of them. I actually threw up, the first time I'd ever been sick on a boat. Perhaps it was stress?

We approached Suva at night and I'd lined up what I thought were some leading lights to take us through the pass in the coral reef protecting Suva Harbour. We were sailing very slowly but my anxiety increased somewhat when one of the lights suddenly drove off. I had obviously fixed on the wrong lights but luck was with me and in the first rays of dawn light, I was able to make out the entrance pass marked rather conspicuously with a small rusty ship, up high and dry on the reef. We might have arrived in the middle of the night had I not sailed too far south, so there was something of a blessing in my faulty navigation after all.

Eventually I traced my navigation anomalies to a big box of tools and spares which I had stowed at the foot of the port quarter berth. This put it just two feet from my main steering compass and was causing some degrees of deviation. It was clearly the reason why we kept finding ourselves off to the portside of where we were heading, such as the unexpected arrival in the vicinity of Late Island, instead of Vava'u. It was also why we missed the lights in the Lau Group as we'd sailed too far to the east.

Clearance into Fiji was relatively simple, but the next day we had to do the rounds of Government Offices. Each department required us to fill out three or four forms in triplicate or quadruplicate with sheets of carbon paper in between. Having five people on board creates a bit of extra writing as all their names have to be entered over and over. Being a single hander has some merits.

Suva is quite a civilised city with a good range of shops, but the anchorage just off one of the main concrete wharves is not conducive to relaxation. We chose not to anchor amongst all the yachts off the Suva Yacht Club finding a quieter spot near the now closed Tradewinds Resort, with *Nanook* alongside. It was an easy bus ride four or five kilometres into Suva from there.

My knee had become swollen and was causing me some difficulty and Cynthia needed treatment for her ear infection. We arrived early one morning at the Suva Hospital Outpatients Department. Our ticket placed us 97th in the waiting queue. The waiting area was filled with all sorts of people, some with tiny crying babies. It was quite an education. Finally after four or five hours we were called into a small bare concrete cubicle to see the doctor. Cynthia received a bag of antibiotic tablets. The doctor examined my knee took a square cotton pad from a shelf, and proceeded to butter it with a black substance that looked like Vegemite and smelt like hot bitumen. He then put this smelly poultice on my knee and bandaged it on telling me to leave it for a few days. I re-fastened my trousers and we were on our way. A few days later, when I removed the bandage my knee was cured.

Greg insisted we attend to my split water tank. Both stainless steel tanks hold around 43 gallons. The split tank on the port side is squat and lies under the galley preparation area, tucked in beside the stove. The tank under the bunk opposite is long and low and the baffles obviously do a better job of taming the contents than they do in the other tank. Getting it out required us to cut away the galley front for access. We took the tank to a welder in Lami, an industrial suburb on the bus route into Suva. The welding shop appeared incredibly primitive and lacking in equipment but the welder did a beautiful job also cutting down the height of the tank by about six inches as I had asked. Greg and I re-installed it and there were no more problems.

We made an excursion on a bus from Suva into the hinterland and some sort of national park, Col-I-Suva, where there was a beautiful mountain pool and a rope to swing out on before dropping down into the cool water. The children and the adults loved it. The next day Paul Coonan and our boys, Douglas and Brian went back to the park for a repeat visit. It was a little stressful letting them go off on their own.

We decided that it was time to leave Suva and explore the islands to the west of Fiji, with the intention of clearing customs from the port of Lautoka on the West Coast. We went to the markets near the waterfront to stock up on kava, which we were told was required to be presented to the chiefs on each of the islands we visited. We bought a supply of Fijian pineapples which were quite small but very sweet and flavoursome.

Kava is the root of some plant which has to be pounded to a powder. It is placed in a cheese cloth and water is squeezed through to make a big bowl of a greyish dishwater looking liquid. The folk of Fiji love it. They say alcohol makes you want to fight whereas kava takes the fight out of you. The stuff doesn't taste bad, not good but not all that bad and definitely better than it looks. It anaesthetises you from the neck down making movement of your limbs slow and cumbersome.

We left Suva for our first stopover at the island of Mbengga to the south west. The main bay here is a deep inlet and is the breeched crater of a long extinct volcano.

We presented our kava to the village chief and were invited to a kava drinking ceremony. I guess it's any excuse for a chance to drink kava. The ceremony follows a strict ritual where everyone sits in a circle and the drinking bowl, a half coconut shell is passed around in the group in an ordered pattern. Many in the circle do clapping which has some meaning in the number of claps and the pace of its rhythm. It seemed like a kind of morse code. Fijians usually nod off after a while at a kava drinking ceremony.

Our kids had a lot of fun running around with the island children and every evening a big group of island men, back from whatever work they do, had a furious game of football. Greg and I spent a few hours trying to fix an outboard engine for some locals and left, fortunately, before the owners were able to test it out.

We sailed around to the other side of Mbengga and anchored off the uninhabited side of an island, Yanutha, inside the big surrounding coral reef. We then left to sail across the bottom of Viti Levu for the drier west coast which is more touristy. Most of the resorts are on the nearby islands and dotted around the southwest and south coasts of Viti Levu.

We made an overnight sail to Malolo Lai Lai, during which a coastal freighter came worryingly close to check us out.

Beachcomber, Fiji 1986 (photo by Greg Coonan)

There are two resorts and an airfield here on Malolo Lai Lai. One is Dick's Place owned by an Australian ex-pat yachtie, Dick Smith. Musket Cove Yacht Club is based here and for $1 you can join the Club, receive a burgee and have your yacht's name carved into the rafters of the bar. For your membership you can use all the facilities, water skiing, wind surfing and the swimming pool at no cost. Our children had a great time.

From there we headed north to the Yasawa Group, another string of islands stretching to the north encircling the North West corner of Viti Levu. At one of our early stops we went ashore and found the islanders putting on a show for a visiting cruise ship. The Blue Lagoon Cruise ships are relatively small with perhaps one hundred and fifty passengers maximum. This particular cruise ship had a large contingent from Fort Worth, Texas, and they invited us to stay to watch the evening's entertainment of dancing and fire activities put on by the islanders.

I noticed Greg and Ann chatting to a rather tall strapping island girl named Evelyn and aged about sixteen. When we left the next day she was aboard *Nanook*. She offered to show us the caves on an island further up the chain. These caves are deep inside the island and to get to some you have to take a deep breath, a leap of faith, and swim through an underwater passage to come up in a subterranean chamber. There's more light under the water than in the chamber and a float has been put in there to hang on to while exploring.

Walker family aboard *Aragunnu* at Yanutha I. (Photo by Greg Coonan)

We sailed further on to an island with a biggish village. It was at this point that Greg and Ann realised that their passenger who had reached her intended destination, had no intention of getting off and was determined to stay for the return to Australia (or maybe anywhere). Greg and I started to agonise over this. Would the islanders think we were kidnapping her? Would war canoes be pushed off from the shore with spear and shield carrying fierce Fijian warriors aboard out to seek vengeance? It was a worrying day. Finally, a decision was made to approach the island chief and discuss it with him. Unfortunately the chief was sick so Greg spoke to the deputy/assistant chief. He offered to go out to *Nanook* with Greg and have a word with the lass. Evelyn meekly left *Nanook* with the deputy chief and an international crisis was averted by skilled diplomacy. We saw her a few days later on the island at a school games day but she quite deliberately turned away when she saw us. I wonder if she ever did escape?

A group of Fijians invited us to a barbeque on a small uninhabited island nearby. Each yacht had five passengers who seemed to have no barbeque equipment, plates, food or anything except their cheery smiles and laughter. They soon picked cassava, speared a lot of small fish with spears made from sharpened bits of steel reo, cut down coconuts for drinks and cooked the food over a fire. Coconut palm leaves were used for the table and plates and it was just terrific. And of course, no washing up.

The Coonans and Walkers, Yasawa Is. Fiji 1986 (Photo by Greg Coonan)

As the cyclone season was approaching we thought it about time to be heading south. We anchored off Lautoka and explored this busy centre with its sugar mill and big shipping wharves. We bought supplies at a 'hypermarket' which was not unlike a Sydney supermarket.

We decided to risk a second bus trip – this time to Nandi, which is a tourist town near the main airport. We had found some of the bus drivers, especially the Indian ones, just a little cavalier in their regard for their passengers' safety and nervous condition. Generally we were happier when we saw the bus driver was a native Fijian. By the way, the buses have no windows and are open to the weather. The trip to Nandi was to take an hour or more so we were a little concerned when we saw our driver was an Indian. The official ushering people onto the bus assured us that our driver was exemplary in his caution. So assured, we boarded the bus. Our Indian driver proceeded with comfortable speeds, driving carefully and safely. About ten minutes from Nandi, he must have realised that he had been dawdling and put his foot to the floor. I don't know whether people have ever experienced those few seconds of total silence when the vehicle is airborne. We did. It was with slightly shaking legs, sweating palms and dry mouths that we got off that bus. Much to our relief, the driver for our return trip was Fijian and we returned safely to our boats.

Our six weeks in Fiji was over and we left a day later.

Aragunnu in New Zealand

We departed in Malolo Lai Lai at 1715, allowing just enough light for *Aragunnu* to pass through the fringing reef. Both *Aragunnu* and *Nanook* had cleared from Lautoka the previous day but following superstition had waited so as not to leave on a Friday, which is supposed to be bad luck amongst sailors. Neither of us is superstitious but in yachting one should leave nothing to chance.

Nanook followed us next morning. Paul Coonan had arranged some last time with Kate from *Sea Eagle*. Both are fourteen and for each, the other was the first teenager either had met on the cruise. Speaking the same teenage language, they had lots to talk about and both being easygoing types, they got along well.

We estimated that *Nanook* would make the voyage in one and a half days less than the slower *Aragunnu*. This proved correct with passage times of nine days and six hours, and ten days and twenty-one hours respectively.

The trades remained steady for the first few days. A period of calms and a few hours of motoring were followed by brisk westerlies and south westerlies. During the calms the children called us to see a twelve to fourteen foot shark about five feet from our stern. It looked up at us but we had nothing to feed it other than ourselves. I radioed *Nanook* somewhere over the horizon, to report our visitor, only to be informed by Greg that the swim he had been thinking about was now off the agenda.

Closer to New Zealand, *Nanook* encountered some winds of thirty knots. Our winds were a little less. Generally the voyage was an anticlimax to all the tall tales we'd heard in the bar at Dick's Place. Most seemed to think we'd have twenty days of calms and a series of on-the-nose gales. Even the Customs folk in Lautoka thought my conservative sixteen day estimate too quick. The dreadful forebodings vanished as the Bay of Islands opened before us with no wind and glassy seas. The penguins ducked under as we motored by.

Rain poured down as Customs cleared *Aragunnu* on Opua Wharf. Shortly after, we rafted up to *Nanook*. The water was icy and there was a chill in the air noticeable to our unacclimatised bodies after the oppressive heat and humidity of the tropics.

New Zealand had some shocks for us. The falling Aussie Dollar had not been matched by the NZ Dollar and prices were eye opening. Just before our arrival a 10% GST had been added to everything, even second hand goods, so prices on some things were even dearer than in Fiji. Locals assured us that the Bay of Islands, being a tourist centre was especially expensive.

I knew New Zealand was a boating nation but the number of yachts there astounded me.

We decided that we would spend some weeks on a motor tour of the North and South Islands. Logically and cost wise our operations should be centred in Auckland. So after a few days we motored south in brilliant sunshine over mirror-like seas. The intervening days we had spent visiting Paihia for shopping, historic Russell, one of the oldest towns in New Zealand and Kawakaka on the scenic 25 km railway. Our short visit convinced us that the Bay of Islands is one of the great cruising grounds.

Greg and I left our mainsails with a sailmaker in Opua to put third reefs in, so *Nanook* was under jib only and *Aragunnu* with spare main and jib. We expected to take twenty-four hours and planned on staying close together as my charts only went as far as Whangerei. I had made a tracing of Greg's "Approaches to Auckland" and marked in all the lights and so on. Inevitably in the dark we became separated and in the dawn light I could see a group of rocky islets directly ahead. Way off to starboard we could see Rangitoto – an island with a volcano – blocking the entrance to Auckland Harbour. We were tired and irritated that the leading lights could not be distinguished from the lights of the city. We furled our sails and motored into the headwinds and chop. By 0920 we had rejoined *Nanook,* patiently waiting for us and found our way up Auckland Harbour to Westhaven Marina. This is a truly enormous marina run by the Harbour Board with over 1400 boats in berths and pile moorings and swinging moorings. To give some idea of the size of this marina, the main arm of the marina, protecting it from the rest of the harbour, has five yacht clubs ranged along it.

After some misunderstandings and foul-ups, we negotiated pile moorings at NZ$16-50 per week and eventually installed ourselves in a spiderwort of lines. Westhaven is a long way from anywhere even though it's in the middle of the city. An expressway cuts it off and it is a very long walk to do some shopping.

Auckland is an attractive city, having some similarities to Sydney with its harbour, bays and bridge, however the water is a dirty brown, perhaps from housing developments up harbour, and lacks any reasonable rivers to flush it out. The weather was a bit miserable while we were there. A strong southwesterly blew continuously. It rains on average 147 days a year and our time there was no exception. The pile berths allowed the rain to blow straight down the companionway so washboards were the order of the day. I managed to have my water tank repaired nearby. The repairs made in Fiji were still good but the tank had split in a different place on the voyage from Fiji.

The two chandlers near Westhaven had outrageous prices and we shrank from proposed alterations, electing to wait until we were back in Sydney.

Westhaven is a showcase for the latest shiny products from the boards of the prolific NZ yacht designers, like Farr, Holland, Young, Lidgard, Davidson, Wright, Townson and other up-and-coming designers, like Elliot. I must confess that slab-sided, flat shear-lined modern cruiser racers with their tall skinny masts and four sets of spreaders leave me cold. I admit they can sail rings around my boat but I do feel they want for aesthetics. A flat line in a design may look modern or fast but a curve is always more attractive to the eye. Still, tastes change and perhaps celebrating my fortieth birthday in November is an indication that I'm not modern anymore. For the purist, many of these yachts are built in cold moulded kauri. We saw one being built this way in Opua.

The Westhaven Yacht Clubs seem to have races every afternoon. Each day there was a procession of yachts leaving the marina. I wondered where all these people find the time for all this sailing and if anyone in Auckland works in the afternoons. They couldn't all be on leave but I guess that it's not the same people sailing every day. It's a fairly upmarket place and yachts belonging to poorer folk are likely kept elsewhere.

We hired a six berth motorhome for 18 days after flying to Christchurch, and all ten of us crowded aboard. It had a shower and toilet, but the overcrowding tested the friendship just a little. We explored a lot of the beautiful South Island having a few memorable adventures on the way then caught the ferry back to the North Island for more exploring. New Zealand is indeed an exceptionally lovely country. Arriving back in Auckland, the Coonans and the Walkers kept apart for a couple of days and the friendship remained intact with irritations forgotten.

Loaded with stores and water, we set out for Great Barrier Island across the Hauraki Gulf. The island is about thirty-five kilometres long and about fifteen wide. It is mostly forested and mountainous, cut into by deep bays and harbours with many small islands along its western shore. Its population of over 800 people live mostly on farms, in small communities, and in communes. Port Fitzroy is the name of the principal harbour and "town" which as far as I could see has one house, a post office, a toilet block-sized building labelled 'library' and a wharf with fuel facilities. Like so much of NZ, the cruising in this area is superb. The anchorages were mostly deserted although we were told 600 or more yachts and power boats are there over Christmas and Easter.

In a small bay at the northern end of the island we were looking for a spot to anchor. On the wharf I could see a large sign with the word "WARNING" at the top but the writing below that was obscured by garbage bins. We anchored and I rowed in to see what the sign said. As I read it there was a thunderous noise and behind me a small amphibious seaplane (a high winged twin engine Grumman type - a Widgeon or a Gosling) landed and shot past *Aragunnu* and up onto a concrete pad where it turned around to go back into the water. The sign was a warning not to anchor in the bay as it was used by seaplanes for landing.

We teamed up with Ray and Cheryl, a Kiwi couple with children, on their 52 foot ferro-cement yacht. At Nagle Cove in Port Abercrombie, Ray had collected over 100 scallops and lunch was held on the poop deck of *Sudden Impulse*. In the following days, we noticed many of the yachts around Great Barrier Island were ferro-cement with a sprinkling of Wharram cats. That night, we anchored off Orama Christian Community. Here is a virtually self-supporting rehabilitation centre set at the end of a long bay and surrounded by high wooded hills. Cynthia purchased bread (frozen) and ice creams from their store and fresh vegetables from their garden. Some seventy or more people live there.

The next day, *Aragunnu* motored back to Smokehouse Bay so as to be able to lie alongside some piles for a scrub. With a reasonable tidal range, these free grids are quite common in NZ and probably save yachts people money from not having to pay slipping fees. The tide was right and we were on the opposite side to a NZ H28, a type which can be seen everywhere. *Zaidar,* belonging to Jim and Eileen mentioned earlier, was one. The single-handed owner was a retired man who had recently taken up yachting. His life seemed to have been a sad one as he confessed to a life spent in the fast lane, spending all his time and money gambling. He thought he would soon swallow the anchor as yachting was too slow and more than likely didn't give him the rush he got from gambling. He'd wintered at Great Barrier Island and we didn't envy that as it was remarkably chilly with the water much too cold for swimming even in December. Crowds of people arrived in Smokehouse Bay and the smokehouses were soon crammed with dozens of big fish, mostly snapper. Thirty teenaged children camped on the beach.

Smokehouse Bay is an area set aside and maintained for boating people. Besides three smokehouses, it has a barbeque, a toilet, a rope swing, washing tubs and wringers, a clothesline and a bathhouse with hot water from a chip heater and the grid on the foreshore. The folk using the smokehouses generously offered us the fish heads straight from the smokehouse. These were big snapper and there was a lot of meat just on the heads, so our stomachs were soon bloated from the volume of delicious freshly smoked fish we consumed.

We scrubbed *Aragunnu* and touched up her antifouling. *Nanook* took our place on the grid, waiting for the next tide. Unfortunately, *Sudden Impulse* had gearbox trouble and, sadly, we farewelled them when they left for Whangarei. The following day the crew of *Nanook* dinghied up a creek to visit a commune and the intermittent rain kept us aboard *Aragunnu.*

Next we visited Whangaparapara Harbour to the south of Port Fitzroy. This used to be a whaling station some decades back, using a converted Fairmile launch as a whale chaser. Now it is a sleepy collection of houses around a wharf with a guest house at its centre. As it was somewhat exposed, we pushed on to Tryphena Harbour, which seemed to be the most populous and civilised part of the island. A cargo boat unloads cars and other goods onto a ramp in one corner and many houses ring the beach-lined bays. Several shops have quite comprehensive ranges of commodities. There are fishing boats and yachts moored in the bays. Proximity to Auckland may be the reason for the popularity of this end of the island. Vast areas of yellow sand are exposed by the retreating three metre tide.

The next day we left for the twenty-five mile crossing of the Hauraki Gulf to Kawau Island. All day the wind remained in the south-east, making an easy reach for us. The island is roughly circular with a two miles deep inlet on its western side, facing towards the main North Island. The steep sides are clad in fir and pine trees and with rocky shores, reminded me of photos I'd seen of Canada or Maine, USA. Each fine day was followed by three or four windy and intermittently wet days. I can see why folk from the British Isles feel at home there. NZ is apparently the largest per capita importer of British manufactured goods. Although funnily enough, Greg and I both observed that NZ radio disk jockeys cultivate Australian accents.

Mansion Bay, at the entrance to Bon Accord Harbour on Kawau Island, has what was once the home of Sir George Grey, one time Governor of South Australia and twice Governor of New Zealand as well as Premier of New Zealand. He cultivated much imported flora and introduced peacocks and wallabies to the surrounding forests. We did a tour of the historic Mansion House with all its antique furniture and walked over part of the island to visit a disused copper mine.

With fifty-four miles to our next anchorage we left at 0730 the next morning for Tutukaka. We bypassed Whangerei as it is a dozen miles up a river estuary, and since we were now day-hopping up the coast, it seemed a waste of a day. Tutukaka Harbour is quite small and the anchorage lies just inside a series of rocky islets that damp out the swell entering the harbour. Whangamumu Harbour was next, a further twenty-five miles on. We had brisk north-easterlies to provide us with a fast sail. If Whangamumu was in New South Wales it would be jammed with waterfront houses and boats but it has three unobtrusive villages and we saw only one other boat.

Whangaruru Harbour is a smallish circular bay with the ruins of an old whaling station, with contented cows grazing amongst the overgrown vats and rusting ironwork. It was just a lunch stop and we soon rounded Cape Brett and entered the Bay of Islands, once more.

Nanook and *Aragunnu* lay rafted together in Deep Water Cove on the same day that NZ Prime Minister Lange was entertaining Australian Government Opposition Leader Bill Hayden, fishing in the Bay of Islands. We didn't see them and I suspect they didn't see us. New Zealand turned on its best weather with a hot sun, a gentle breeze, and a bright blue sky with a smattering of gentle puffs of cloud. The sun was intense and we all sunburned easily and had headaches.

Many boats had arrived in the Bay since our earlier departure, including some of our acquaintances from the tropics. *Iemanje* from Brittany, who we had anchored near at the Tradewinds in Fiji, had escaped a cyclone and arrived with a fourth crewmember born in Suva Hospital. We sat on the beach at Roberton Island and swapped stories of our respective passages. Then we found Brett and Trish with *Shaula* on the slip and up for sale. We'd become good friends since meeting them in Tonga and later in Fiji. Their Southern Hemisphere circumnavigation via Magellan Straits had taken five years and they were at a loose end as to what to do next. Another larger vessel seemed the way to go. I imagine that after so long away from home and such adventures, settling down on land is difficult, perhaps impossible and all that is left is to keep sailing.

We received the sad news that Eric Hiscok had died in September. We didn't see *Wanderer IV* or Susan Hiscock, although the Hiscocks have been a tourist attraction in the Bay for yachties.

We took a rising tide up the twisting river to Kerikeri Basin. *Nanook* sat on the mud for a short while but the rising tide soon lifted her off. The Basin is tiny and crowded with moorings, but worth the visit in attractiveness and history. The main town is a twenty-minute walk away; however the supermarket there is much cheaper than elsewhere in the Bay area. An old timer described the famous 1981 flood and showed us where the water had risen to, many feet above our heads where we were standing on the quay. A ferro boat was tied up there with its owner waiting (something yachtsmen do a lot of) for a starter motor to be repaired and a girlfriend to arrive from Fiji. When we left, at least the starter motor had arrived.

A couple of days later, we anchored in Opua. The moorings were full of international yachts. We imagined it was more like being moored in Long Beach California or somewhere like that with all the big shiny American yachts. During the night, the tail of a tropical cyclone lashed the bay around the back of Russell, where we were anchored. The yachts anchored downwind of us shouted out the weather forecast to us and were concerned that we would drag down on them. I put out our 35lb plow anchor on 110 feet of chain and our 22lb Bruce anchor on rope and chain all in fifteen feet of water. I felt we'd be pretty safe. Greg had trouble setting his 27lb plow but was finally satisfied. It was hard to sleep that night with the wind rattling the mast and sending shivers through the boat, heeling us first one way then the other. The boats nearby were bucking up and down from wind-blown waves. The gusts were at least 35 knots over the deck. We were thankful not to be in a more exposed place. It was comforting to know *Nanook* was anchored a couple of boat lengths to starboard. Late the next afternoon, Greg thought it prudent to move to a more sheltered location but suffered engine problems and had to anchor twice more before finding somewhere reasonably protected. The anchoring had been tricky in a few places and both of us had trouble at various times. Greg became less emphatic about the merits of different anchor types. (I overheard him offering one of his cheaply.) It is always interesting to listen to the controversies amongst yachties. Fixed narrow views were offered on the merits of CQR versus Bruce, full keel versus fin, fractional rig versus masthead, multihull versus mono, comfort versus speed and so on. I know where I stand, but I may change and I realise everyone comes from a different situation, so I prefer not to get into these sorts of arguments. I also dislike anyone being the arbiter of taste for others and of course, no single truism suits everyone.

The days left before our departure were racing. Newly-wed friends from Sydney paid us a visit and we pumped them for news from back home.

Then it was Christmas. We celebrated with roast chicken, baked potatoes, peas, gravy and all the trimmings and later, plum pudding with cream and custard. Santa Claus was sympathetic to our situation and the presents were few, inexpensive and compact. Curious!

The Northland Harbour Board introduced a NZ$50 once only fee for yachts entering the ports under their control. Most considered this fee exorbitant and many were refusing to pay. The French boats paid as they thought the fee was for French boats only – perhaps to cover surveillance costs as the *Rainbow Warrior* incident was not too long ago and New Zealand's suspicion of the French was still strong. The $50 was widely regarded as a rip-off and statutory fundraiser. So we spent our time dodging the Harbour Master and not flying our national flag as well as keeping clear of Opua. Eventually we decided it would be cheaper to clear from Whangarei (also N.H.B.), so we headed south again.

Just before leaving I had my first "brush with fame". On the watering barge in Otehei Bay was an American yacht from Miami, Florida. Its owner told me his name: Andy Wall, and that he was an Australian. He mentioned his first boat *Carronade* and I made the connection. Andy, with his friends, Des Kearn*s*, Ken Mills and Bill Nance sailed *Carronade,* a 31 foot Carmen class yacht

(*Cadence* a Carmen class, won the Sydney to Hobart in 1966) made in Australia, across the Pacific, around Cape Horn and up the Atlantic to the USA in 1964-9. There was another Nance brother, Bill, who didn't sail with Andy and was in the Guinness Book of Records for some years for sailing a 25 foot Vertue Class yacht *Cardinal Vertue* single-handed around Cape Horn in 1963. *Cardinal Vertue* had been sailed by Dr. David Lewis in the first single-handed Transatlantic Race in 1960 and he sold it to Bill Nance. I believe that in more recent times, somebody wind-surfed around Cape Horn after launching from a powerboat. Andy's present boat, which I was looking at, is a GRP Halvorsen designed Freya Class made in the USA. The original *Freya* won the Sydney to Hobart Race three times in 1963, 1964 and 1965. Travelling with Andy were his American wife, Pam (the reason he stayed in the USA) and their two children. I told him I'd read Des Kearns book of their voyage.

The sail south was a misery, with a very potent sun mercilessly beating down and wind on the nose at five knots. There were dozens of yachts going the other way to spend their Christmas-New Year break in the Bay of Islands. Some 2000 boats go there at this time of the year. We overnighted at crowded Tutukaka and caught up with our friends on *Sudden Impulse*. Early next morning, we pushed on to Whangerei, which lies twelve miles inland up a river. It is the principal town in the northern end of New Zealand's North Island. The river yacht basin was crowded and it was the Harbour Master's day off, so we escaped wharfage fees and the iniquitous entry fee. Customs clearance was friendly and painless. Ann and Cynthia discovered the cheapest supermarket, possibly in all of the North Island, only a short walk from the wharf. By 1630, we were on our way again. With the wind still on the nose, we anchored in a small bay near the river mouth. Over the next two days, *Aragunnu* motored and sailed to Cape Reinga at the northernmost tip of New Zealand. *Nanook* over-nighted a couple of times on the way. We finally passed the Cape at 0500 on January 1st. In a rising south-easterly, we shot like a cork from a bottle through the gap between the Cape and Three Kings Islands. The wind held for some days and the miles rattled off. We caught a four or five kilo tuna on the trailing line - the first for the entire trip, then immediately caught another smaller one, which we regretfully let go. Soon we were back to standard boat fare of rice, boiled cabbage and carrots, tinned corn beef, mutton or tuna, sometimes curried for variety. Our thoughts were of getting home.

By mid-Tasman, *Aragunnu* was to be found sitting at the centre of a vast flat plain of dark blue, topped by a dome of clear pale blue, and with the sun shining down. On board was the steady throb of the diesel. The fresh air in the cabin was replaced by diesel fumes and the smell of hot engine oil. I wished my entreaties to the Almighty for a calm passage had not been so insistent. At that moment I would have sold my soul to the devil for fifteen knots of north-easterly. In the brief thunder squall that followed I tried to remember whether Faust got out of it or not.

Impediments to progress produced irritation. Both yachts encountered a wicked little contrary current that took twenty miles a day off our progress as we closed the coast. Passing through the same area on the outward passage, it probably accounted for a remarkable 150 mile day we had. The night watches were the worst. We saw at least one ship per day in these last days and so needed to maintain vigilance. For Cynthia and me, it was very tiring. The days were too hot to sleep and the children were effervescent with the prospect of being home and with friends again.

At last we passed through Sydney Heads at 0315 on the 11th January. *Nanook* arrived six hours before us. We had been gone six months, spent fifty-one days at sea and covered 5,300 ocean miles.

Doug's Journal

When we left on our South Pacific Cruise, our oldest son, Douglas, was almost nine and a half years old. As he would be out of school for six months, we suggested that, as part of his educational program supervised by his teacher Mother, he keep a journal. Brian at seven years of age also kept a journal, but this has not survived. Douglas and Brian received an educational program of tasks, tailored to their respective ages and set by their mother. Jane at four years of age, had not yet started school and so received a level of tuition appropriate to her age.

With Douglas' permission his journal is reproduced below. I have included the journal in its entirety, although perhaps too long and a little tedious to an adult reader, it shows the day-to-day minutiae of the voyage as seen through the eyes of a nine and a half year old boy. I have made a few corrections to improve clarity but have tried to preserve Doug's language and creative spelling. It also demonstrates Douglas' development as a diarist.

Douglas, now 44 years old, with a wife and two children, a responsible job with the Union Sanitary District of California, USA, and two Masters Degrees, was always able to move forward, learning from the lessons of life, developing into a mature and confidant man. I like to think that our voyage, in some way, contributed to that.

Tonga Thursday 7th August 1986

We spotted Late Is, in the early hours of the morning thinking it was Vavau. Late Is. is very interesting because you could see the crater inside. Slowly we reached sight of Vavau. We gradually got closer and our friends on board Nanook came out to meet us. We anchored in a sheltered bay called Port Maurelle. The water in the bay was clear and easy to see the anchor drop the thirty feet into the water. We left every thing how it was (in a mess) and rowed ashore for a run. We ate pineapple and coconut, the juice was delicious and the coconut was not bad either. It felt funny to walk on land again after being at sea for 26 days in mainly rough or becalmed weather. When we got back to the boat I bet my parents felt good to have a sleep without getting up for midnight watches.

Tonga Friday 8th August 1986

We were woken early by an erge for an early morning swim. The water was cold at first but warm after a while. We were in swimming for half an hour when we got out we had weetbix, milk and sugar. Then we went to the capital at Neiafu for customs. We rowed ashore and walked to the customs office in a shed. They said "Tie up to the wharf" but my father objected so we walked to the Immigration Centre but they said the same. So we went back to the wharf where some men came and said they'd catch the ropes. So we rowed to the boat and motored gently in to the wharf. The police and the man in charge of the customs shed came aboard. Then we went to the bank where I raced back to the boat and got my mother's passport. I made it back because there were about 30 people in each line. Then we bought ice-creams. We went shopping while my father booked us up for dinner. We finally finished shopping and we carried them to the dinghy where we rowed to the boat. The two families had a swim for an hour but I got out half an hour before the others to get ready. We found out that the motor didn't work so we were towed by "Nanook" using their motor. We got there a bit too late. The dinner was delicious. For dessert we had cake. On the way back the water was fluorescent and we had to watch out for mooring lines.

Tonga Saturday 9th August 1986

At 7.00 my mother went to the market to buy provisions for us. Then while everyone was on our boat we went to get water where Joanne had a shower and my mother and Ann did the washing. Then we dropped the Coonans off at their boat and motored through coral, my mother was lookout. We stopped at Ano Beach where we went swimming and my mother went ashore and I went to Nanook and played a game of chess. Then my father called Paul and I to come ashore where I bought a $3-00 carving. I also saw Tongan dancing. Then we went back to the boat where my mother fixed our net and we went to bed.

Tonga Sunday 10th August 1986

We got up early and went swimming in Nanooks dinghy. We capsized it, got in it and fell out again. We were in all morning and when we got out it was lunch. We had lunch on Nanook and then we played in the dinghy again. Then we got out and got ready to go ashore for jaffles and toast along with *Silver Cloud, Taurangi, Herman, Nanook* and us. We had great fun. Then we went back to the boat and got ready for bed and went to bed.

Tonga Monday 11th August 1986

We woke at a reasonable time and went for a quick swim because it was very hot and I was sunburnt. Then I got out and did a lot of schoolwork. Then we had lunch and my mother and sister went ashore and when they came back Paul was with them so Paul picked us up and went to *Nanook* for games of chess. I beat him using three pieces and the time two pieces another two pieces and the last game he won. Then I went back to our boat and had a swim, I got out had dinner and went to bed early.

Tonga Tuesday 12th August 1986

I was woken early by the pattering of rain on the roof of the fore-cabin. I got up and found that Dad was collecting water because the Neiafu water was foul.

I went for a swim. The water was cool!!!. I practised swimming properly for I hadn't done it for a while. Then we cut up paw-paw. Ann invited us over for pikelets, we accepted the offer. We left half an hour after the offer. The pikelets were delicious but hot. We had about 20 then left for *Taurangi*. We played games like chess, checkers and snakes and ladders. We then left to go back to our boat for dinner then paw-paw and fruit cake. We listened to Penta Comstat but we turned it off and went to bed.

Tonga Wednesday 13th August 1986

I got up late because I had a sleep in. I went for a swim as usual and found out that I wasn't sunburnt anymore. We got out and had porridge. We went ashore to catch the bus into Neiafu. The hours were ticking away. We finally reached the bus stop and no bus came. So we walked on and a truck came by and picked us up. The ride took only about ten minutes. When we got there we went to the market and got lunch for one dollar fifty. We went to the post office and spent nearly $10 on stamps. Then we went to the bank to get some more money out. We then got an ice cream and walked to the school and my mother started joking about joining me to the Tongan school. Then we went to the bus stop to catch the bus back. We caught it and left, it took about ten minutes and walked the rest of the way. Then we used the outboard to get to the boat. For dinner we had bread. We went to bed early because we were tired.

Tonga Thursday 14th August 1986

We woke up early for a swim and Greg came over and discussed about changing bays. We changed to Taunga because we didn't want to stay in the same bay the whole time. We anchored in two metres of water. We had a swim and it was easy to see the bottom even touch it. We rowed ashore and walked along the white sandy beach and went body surfing on the sand bar where big waves rolled us off the other edge. We then left because a storm was nearing. We had dinner and went to bed because it was late. Greg, Ann, Mum and Dad played eucre and opened a bottle of baileys.

Tonga Friday 15th August 1986

We woke early and went for a swim while Kevin from *Scorpio III* came over with his wife for a haircut. He also invited us to come ashore for lunch. We had fish and jaffles. We then went for a walk to the village and bought some items like shell mats and when we came back some Tongans followed us back and when we got back they made sand castles and listened with curiosity to our chat. We then left had dinner and went to bed.

Tonga Saturday 16th August 1986

In the morning we noticed that Kevin had moved, he invited my parents plus Greg and Ann over for tea and coffee. The wind picked up and my parents returned to leave for Port Maurelle for shelter from the wind. After half an hour we saw the Coonans rounding the point. We decided to raft up. The others walked to the village except Joanne and I. When they came back we had a dinner together with lemon tart and banana crumble for dessert.

Tonga Sunday 17th August 1986

In the morning Paul and I played a few games of chess and draughts. My mother made pikelets for the two families for lunch then we went for a walk to the other village. We picked pretty shells then we left. I found two pretty shells on the way back. We had dinner then played games of euchre because my mother taught us how to play then we went to bed.

Tonga Monday 18th August 1986

Paul and Ann came over and we cast off from *Nanook* to go to Neiafu for water and supplies. We tied up to Colemans wharf and filled up with water. My mother and Ann went shopping.

Paul went to Tili's house for a carving. He saw my mum on the way back and helped carry things to Colemans wharf. We rafted up to Nanook at 4.00, had dinner and went to bed.

Tonga Tuesday 18th August 1986

Desiderata came over with monopoly, the game stopped because Joanne stole money from the bank. For the rest of the day we played chess, draughts and backgammon had dinner and went to bed.

Tonga Wednsday 20th August 1986

Silver Cloud anchored in Port Maurelle along with *Taurangi*. Today is very hot and I did a lot of swimming.

Tonga Thursday 21st August 1986

It was so hot we did swimming all day. In the evening we had a happy hour and most of the people came.

Tonga Friday 22nd August 1986

We went to Neiafu in the morning and did some shopping. We went to *Morris Hedstrom* to talk with Fefita's husband and he took us to his house we watched a video with John Wayne as the star. Then we went back to the boat and played games then we had dinner and had an early night.

Tonga Saturday 23rd August 1986

We went to *Morris Hedstrom* and saw Fefita and brought her back to the boat We had ice cream that she gave us, it was delicious. Then we had lunch and went shopping. Then we left to go to Hunga. We got there late in the afternoon and Greg and Ann came out to meet us for the rest of the day. We played, had dinner and went to bed.

Tonga Sunday 23rd August 1986

We went ashore and stayed there the whole day. Then we went back had dinner and went to bed.

Tonga Monday 24th August 1986

At 12 midnight my mother woke us up and took us to see Moses and *Rambo*. We didn't see Moses or *Rambo*. We saw *Ben Hur* and they stopped half way through. We left and went to bed again. We woke up late and went ashore and asked the man to put on Rambo he arranged at 7:00. The day passed slowly finally we saw *Rambo* then we left and went to bed.

Tonga Tuesday 25th August

We went ashore to give Emily a haircut but she refused so we went to the plantation. We left Hunga and motored around with Paul on the surf ski to south Hunga a sheltered bay. We went for a swim and snorkell. We went ashore and played on the sand-bar and we walked around the island. Then we went back had dinner and went to bed.

Tonga Wednesday 27th August 1986

In the morning we played assorted games and after lunch we went to Kenuto and saw the most enormous crayfish everyone took photos. So we went ashore to try our luck in finding one like the other people. We didn't have any luck. Then we went across the reef and saw assorted animals. We then left and had dinner and an early night in the tent.

Tonga Thursday 28th August 1986

When we woke up we played cards. Greg and Bruce swam in and Paul lit the fire but we didn't have breakfast on shore. We had Weet-bix and sugar. Swimming all day and had lunch and went swimming. *Silver Cloud* and *Nanook* had dinner on shore. We had dinner on the boat and went to bed.

Tonga Friday 29th August 1986

We walked on the southern reef and did a lot of swimming all day and had dinner together and went to bed.

Tonga Saturday 30th August 1986

Swimming a lot. We had pikelets on shore for lunch made baskets. Swam out to the boat. Had dinner and the adults learnt tripolly.

Tonga Sunday 31st August 1986

We went to Taunga to have a look. We went to Nuku. We stayed at Port Maurelle for that night.

Tonga Monday 1st September 1986

We did a lot of swimming and in the afternoon Brian and I went to Neiafu on *Nanook*. When we got there Greg rammed a fishing boat but they didn't mind. Ann hopped off and went to the post office and bank. We saw *Aragunnu* and hopped back on board.

Tonga Tuesday 2nd September 1986

We got up early and started walking into town because of the Agricultural Show. It was a long walk and luckily a man with a van picked all ten of us up and took us to town. The show was at the high school which Japan gave them. We looked at the exhibits Then the King of Tonga came in his open army vehicle in his ski boots. We then sat down and watched. We then left and looked at the exhibits and stinking fish. When we got back my mother had got coffee and cake for nothing. When the King left the show finished and it started to pour. We walked back to Neiafu and to Robyn's for hamburgers and banana split, an afternoon treat.

Tonga Wednesday 3rd September 1986

We went ashore to clear customs and post letters and get groceries. We then left and anchored in Port Maurelle, a favoured spot by all of us.

Tonga Thursday 4th September 1986

In the morning we had a last swim and prepared for the trip across. We left at 11 o'clock and by late afternoon we were off Late Is.

Pacific Ocean Friday 5th September 1986

We missed the light on the island and had gone too far south. So we headed north, the Trade-winds steadily pushing us N West. My mother still had the sore throat.

Pacific Ocean Saturday 6th September 1986

We missed the light on Totoya and in the morning we saw islands. My mother still had her sore throat and now it was worse.

Pacific Ocean Sunday 7th September 1986

Today Father's Day and Dad had to do all the work. My mother was still sick and thought she wouldn't be able to do night watches.

Fiji Monday 8th September 1986

At 6 o'clock we saw the lights of Suva but it took two hours till we were in Suva Harbour. We anchored next to *Nanook* and waited... After 5 hours we were fed up and contacted *Nanook*. They saw the boat and made it come to us. When they finished we tied up to the wharf and cleared. Then we went ashore and walked around Suva. We had dinner at a Chinese restaurant. The restaurant was great and the food delicious.

Fiji Tuesday 9th September 1986

When I woke up I thought I was back in Sydney. We went to clear agriculture and Mum and Jane went to the hospital. We had lunch and Brian, Jane and Mum went back to the hospital. We found out that we had received mail from home. I saw big buildings and heaps of people from India, Fiji and China. We went back to the boat had dinner and went to bed early.

Fiji Wednesday 10th September 1986

We rang Grandma again and us kids spoke. Then we motored to the Trade Winds Hotel in the blinding rain. We also got the tank out for repair. Walked into Lami to a welder called Barney. *Nanook* stayed in Suva.

Fiji Thursday 11th September 1986

Dad walked into Lami and bought 10 scones, 2 for each of us before *Nanook* came around. Nanook arrived at lunchtime. We saw our first seasnake and I thought I'd never swim in Fiji. Yves, Brigette and Mirrodyn from *Iejmanje* were the first French people we've met on the cruise.

Fiji Friday 12th September 1986

We played assorted games all day cause of the rain and Bruce gave the tank to Barney for repairs. It will take one week to fix.

Fiji Saturday 13th September 1986

The rain stopped and Greg, Bruce, Paul, Brian and I walked into Lami and had a look at the boat shop. We got a couple of brochures and potted around.

When we got back we had lunch and played games on *Nanook*.

Fiji Sunday 14th September 1986

We walked into Lami and decided to walk into Suva so we walked and walked... While Brain and Dad stayed at the boat. We walked to the Royal Suva Yacht Club and Paul caught a bus back because we were going to the barbeque that they were putting on. Paul got back in half an hour and we had hamburgers and watched the Cowra Breakout where the Japs fort the Aussies. Then a blackout came and we were in total black for 15 minutes. Then the power came on again and the Cowra Breakout finished and we left.

Fiji Monday 15th September 1986

We just sat around and Greg caught a bus into town.

Fiji Tuesday 16th September 1986

All ten of us left early to go to Col-I-Suva to the pools, so we caught a bus into Suva where Greg and Dad were waiting. We waited 5 minutes till the bus came. We all hopped aboard and grabbed a seat. The trip to the bus stop took 10 minutes and there we caught a taxi for a 3 minute $2 trip down to the track to the upper pools. We found a picnic area where we had lunch and met the ranger of that area. When we finished lunch we started walking along the long…long track. It took 15 minutes to get to the upper pools. We had a swim and Dad kept asking where the rope was. We had our photo taken under waterfall on the rocks. We got dressed and walked down to the lower pools where the rope was. We met some people from Canada and we saw some Fijians swinging. Paul decided to go first then Brian then I. I swang and I was only scared when I was about 3 metres above water level and about to fall, when I hit the water. My cossies came up my bum which I hated. My mother was really scared about my going on the swing but she regained her confidence in me enough to let Jane go from the beginners ledge. My four year old sister wasn't scared at all and these Canadian girls were and they were in there twenties! We each had approximately 20 go's then we left and walked to the forest station where we caught a bus back into Suva where we saw Liz and Lou on *Silver Cloud* who took 5 days to get here.

We asked them out for a curry but they said no because they wanted rest because of the trip here. The curry was very very hot and I ate a lot. Then we went for chocs and ice-creams at the Pizza Place. Then we caught the bus back to the Trade-Winds. We rowed out and went straight to bed.

Fiji Wednesday 17th September 1986

Brian, Bruce and I went ashore and waited for the tank. When we got it we went out and left for Suva to fill the water tank. We picked up Ian from Iron Butterfly and took him in. Brian helped fill the tank. And then Mum and me went to the hospital because my Dad had a sore knee and us kids played on *Nanook*. When Dad came back he had to go back on Friday so we went back to the Trade-Winds.

Fiji Thursday 18th September 1986

We played euchre and the adults were thinking about letting us go to Col-I-Suva by ourselves. In the end they said yes. So we started packing fruit, biscuits and towels, finally we left with my mother but she didn't come. She left at Suva. We caught the long bus ride to the beginning of the track, further than before by Paul's decision. We walked and walked past the 2 upper pools and straight to the more fun lower pools and swing. I felt more confident in myself being almost alone. Finally my legs started getting tired but we were getting closer, I could tell.

When we got there Paul jumped for the rope and got it. I had first go and the water was freezing but I didn't mind. It's about six metres deep so it's nothing to be scared about

We were having great fun. Meanwhile on the boat Mum was shopping with Greg, Ann, Leigha. Bruce was resting his swollen knee as the doctor said. . .

Col y Suva swimming hole

We finally stopped and had our oranges. Paul and Brian were still swinging. I decided to go in again. I swang out, in , out, in and stopped. I once tried to go from the beginners ledge and dive but I couldn't get my legs up and did a horsey. We finally left after two hours of swinging and falling in the water. We walked along a different trail to the forest station, another of Paul's decisions, on a trail called the Big Pauka trail which is slightly longer than the other trail.

When we reached the village and the football field we waited at the bus stop and counted the money. We caught the bus back to Suva and had fun with a strong breeze on your face. It took 5 minutes. We reached Suva and caught a bus to Trade-Winds.

One was Jeremiah who we played with. We met a man called Joe Ben Bolt a big man. We then learnt how to throw a spear a long way. At first I couldn't throw very far but I got better. Later on, Sevenella came back and the adults came in. We saw them mix the kava powder with water. We even tasted it. It tasted rather horrible. For the rest of the day we through spears. We then went out to the boat.

Fiji Sunday 21st September 1986

It rained most of the day and Jeremiah came out with his friend and had lunch on our boat. When they left we tipped the dinghy. When we tip it we get inside where we can breathe. We also lie ahull where we get the dinghy vertical and stay there. We got out in a hurry to go to church. In church there weren't many people because most people took their children to the other village for school. When church finished Mum and Dad had a cup of tea at Joe's house while I, Paul and Brian practised spear throwing. Now I can through spears very far.

Fiji Monday 22nd September 1986

We swam and tipped the dinghy for most of the day. We went in and watched Greg and Dad help fix an outboard. We also through spears and now I can through about 6 metres. For the rest of the day we tipped the dinghy.

Fiji Tuesday 23rd September 1986

In the morning we motored around to the other side of Mbenga and Dad called me up to see the most enormous turtle we'd ever seen. It stayed up two seconds then dived just after I came up. When we got there we tipped the dinghy and rowed ashore for a swim. Rowed down the creek and met some home coming school children. Then Ann Greg and Mum came in and we met an Aussie lady from Melbourne and she said that the children steal and catch it from their parents. She invited us back tomorrow.

Fiji Wednesday 24th September 1986

The adults and the two littlies went ashore to meet her husband and we stayed and played Tableaunette. When they came back we motored across to Yanutha and anchored in crystal clear water like back in Port Maurelle. I caught up in the journal and went snorkelling. When I got out I had dinner and as we had pineapple my loose molar fell out, my mother put it in a cup of water.

Fiji Thursday 25th September 1986

I got up and went snorkelling. I must have dived up and down more than 100 times to see the beautifully coloured fish that hide amongst the coral reefs. When I come near they all rush into places or cracks I couldn't get to in the assorted colours on the coral heads. I feel as if I'm in a world without sunlight, only the beautiful colours on the coral. I wish I had an air tank and breathing system to see the pretty fish that glide along the bottom of the sea. I found a spider shell that had the original animal inside. Most coloured shells are hidden in the sand close to shore or under coral further out. When I got out I found that my tooth had an Australian 50 cent piece under it. I guess the Tooth Fairy knew what country I come from. We had dinner and went to bed.

Fiji Friday 26th September 1986

We went for our last swim and I went sailing single handed and a gust came and I capsized. Joanne and Brian went in while I snorkelled. When I got out Brian and Paul walked to the village and when they came back we prepared for the trip across to Malolo Lai Lai. After half an hour we left had dinner and went to bed at sea.

Fiji Saturday 27th September 1986

When I woke up we were in sight of Malolo Lai Lai and we sailed through the reef and anchored in 9 metres of water. We went swimming and tipped the dinghy. We were invited over for euchre at *Nanook*. Then we got bored and left. I went for a ski and snorkel but couldn't see the bottom. Then Paul rowed over to the hotel to see the anchorage. It was better than this one. So we moved to the other side of the bay and Jane, Brian and I rowed ashore and I came back to pick up Mum and Dad. When they came in we walked around with the Coonans. We went back had dinner and went to bed.

Fiji Sunday 28th September 1986

I woke up and we went ashore and a swim at the Musket Cove Yacht Club. We also had a barbeque with stake, salad and sauce. We bought three packets of choc chip biscuits. Then we went for a swim. We had a sundae and left. We had cheese on toast for dinner and Brian caught up to date in his journal.

Fiji Monday 29th September 1986

I woke up and caught up in journal. We had delicious creamed rice for breakfast. Then Jane, Brian and I went over and mum and dad came over. Paul, Brian and I learned how to play cut throat euchre. We all went ashore and went swimming at Dick's Place in the pool. We got out and had a sundae. We sat around talking then we had a Rockyroad, a Gaytime in Australia. We went on the surf ski and kayak then we went swimming again and played a game where you through a coin in and jump in after it and whoever gets it gets a point. We got out and left. Went back to the boat had a large meal and went to bed.

Fiji Tuesday 30th September 1986

We got up and Paul, Joanne, Leigha and Ann came and picked us up and took us in. We went swimming in the pool and looked for the big coconut crab that we spotted yesterday. We had an ice cream and went water skiing for the first time. We met Arthur who we invited out for dinner but he got an asthma attack and we went to bed early because of my cold.

Fiji Wednesday 1st October 1986

When I woke up Dad told us it was the first day of the hurricane season. We went ashore and almost walked around the island. We went swimming and we also went on the aquaplane with the 40 horse power. *Shaula* came in and we had a delicious barbeque and Fu Fu caught a coconut crab and I had it for dinner along with stake and salad.

Fiji Thursday 2nd October 1986

Nothing special happened except that my mother caught a sucker fish which looked like a shark. We took photos but then threw it back. Peter from *Emerald City* gave us some corned beef cans. Then we left in the boiling hot sun to Waya Is. It took 6 long hot hours to get there and when we got there it was dinner so we had dinner and played cards.

Fiji Friday 3rd October 1986

We woke up had breakfast and Brian, Jane and I with Leigha rowed ashore. Paul was on the surf ski. We looked for shells like cowries. Then we played cards and started a new game of euchre. We had lunch and moved around to another bay where a man got taken by a shark. We went ashore and looked at the school, even joined in, in a game of football and I hit my head on the ground. We walked to the village with the children. We met a French lady called Mirriam and her baby Stephanie. We went back and went body surfing on the big waves. We had dinner on the boat and went to bed.

Fiji Saturday 4th October 1986

Greg went for a run and gave kava to the chief. We moved around to Turtle Island. Today is very hot. The trip took all day and Greg was zooming ahead with double reefed main and small jib. When we got there two men offered us a $6 lobster, we bought it. Then we played cards on *Nanook*. The lobster was yellow and red after being cooked. It had a lot of meat. I loved it. It was my first lobster I've had in my life and probably my last.

Fiji Sunday 5th October 1986

I woke up and went for a row through the mangroves. When we got back breakfast was ready. We had breakfast and did schoolwork. We went rowing again but with the dinghy danforth. Joanne finished schoolwork and came with us in her dinghy. We both moved in a raft. After lunch we moved around to the other side. We rowed ashore and went swimming. Then the adults came ashore and went for a walk while we made a raft. When we went out to the boat we had a meal together played cards and went to bed.

Fiji Monday 6th October 1986

I woke up and caught up on journal and went for a row with Brian and Jane to shore. When we came back we had breakfast of Weetbix. We potted around on both boats until lunch when I went swimming with the others. Invited Kate from Sea Eagle over and played Tripoly and pontoon. Kate won both games. We went to a "do" and saw dancing. We came back and went to bed.

Fiji Tuesday 7th October 1986

I woke up and did heaps and heaps of schoolwork. Went swimming and snorkelling on the reef. We saw different coral than in other places, beautifully coloured coral that is undestroyed by the 'Crown of Thorns'. We saw the crown of thorns that had been destroying all the coloured coral. We quickly got out had lunch and motored across to the village to give kava and see Evelyn who we met last night. She gave the Coonans shells and paw-paw. We walked around the village then rowed out to the boat with Evelyn in their dinghy. They showed her around their boat while my parents cooked a cake. They took her back and came over for dinner. We had a salad and glazed fruit gateau for dessert. We played cards and went to bed.

Fiji Wednesday 8th October 1986

Because of last night we woke up very late. We went for a row while my mother cooked breakfast then did schoolwork till lunch time. We rowed into shore and started digging a hole, we dug for an hour. Finally we started a sand fight with sand bombs. Some of them hurt but not many. We finally got a rest and the adults came in and walked around the island. After one and a half hours we rowed out and played cards until the adults came out. Then we had dinner and my parents played cards on Nanook and found out we had sunstroke. At 11 o'clock pm my brother got up and was sick all over the head floor. He got in trouble for not doing it in the toilet.

Fiji Thursday 9th October 1986

Greg motored and picked up Evelyn and for the first time we led out through the passage and sailed to the caves. When we anchored Greg was at the village giving kava and asking permission to go to the caves. Then we moved over here still with Evelyn. We waited till the cruise people came out then we moved in. One of the Fijians showed us to the cave and pulled us through the dark cave on the raft. When my eyes got adjusted to the dark I saw a lot more, like the roof and the rocks hanging from the top. Then we saw a shaft of light coming down from a crack in the roof then further on saw a volcano like 'shaft' long and narrow going up to the sunlight. We headed back and got Mum, Dad, Ann, Paul, Leigha and Joanne and Jane who had a lot of trouble getting in, then we all went through seeing the shafts of light and Evelyn climbed out one shaft then we went out and Evelyn showed us where the light was coming in and the one she climbed out. Then we got in and Evelyn showed us the other cave which started from water and went up and came down to water again. When we came out we showed the rest of the group the cave through the entrance we came out. The family and I went through the cave again. We were starting to get a chill so we climbed up the ladder got dressed and left. We saw Ann and Greg on the beach and the adults and Paul talked about movies and videos. Then we bailed the dinghy out and moved over to the other side. Then we had dinner and my parents went to a kava party and we went to *Nanook* and played cards. Then we went to bed.

Fiji Friday 10th October 1986

We were woken early and found out that it was Fiji Day and we rowed ashore and walked to the school to see football, netball, a kava ceremony. For football it was this village and Nandi. This village won in netball. It was the same, the home team won. When we got back we went for an explore up river, then had a look on Sea Eagle. Then we had dinner and went to bed.

Fiji Saturday 11th October 1986

We motored over to the other side and picked up villagers who were going to make a picnic for us. Picking them up in the dinghy was with heaps of waves in the boat. Finally we went to the island we are having it on. Greg got the kasava and cooked it. We had a great meal, fish, coconut, and what we call tapioca, kasava here. Then I made a rowing boat out of coconut palms. I walked half way around the island with Ann and Wesley. Then we walked back and rowed out and motored back and dropped them off. Out of all of them I liked Ben and Simon the best. We anchored near the caves and after dinner we were all so tired we went straight to bed.

Fiji Sunday 12th October 1986

We had breakfast and looked on the cruise ship while Paul set the sailing dinghy up and the others went snorkelling. Then Joanne and I rowed up to Sea Eagle and Paul was sailing. Then he picked up Brian and went sailing with him while Kate, Joanne and I talked. Finally we all came back and while no one was at the caves we went there and took photos breaking a rule. Villagers throught that if photos were taken one person would die. It was great fun in the caves for the last time. Then we went snorkelling for the last time and Joanne and I saw a foot long fish about half a foot high. After dinner Greg and Ann came over and played cards.

Fiji Monday 13th October 1986

We went to the village to say goodbye. We got water and Ben gave us some shell necklaces.

Douglas' Journal ends here.

Before we cruised again, I built and installed a new fibreglass dodger on *Aragunnu* to increase comfort in the cockpit.

Aragunnu with new fibreglass dodger

Island of Dreaming

Lord Howe is the perfect South Seas Island - it's the sort of place where you are reminded of books you read as a child, like *Coral Island*. High, cloud-topped mountains, a fringing coral reef and lagoon, lashings of palm trees and enough yellow sandy beaches to leave a single track of footprints; it has all of this. Perhaps it is because it is 421 miles across unpredictable, open ocean from Sydney, that a visit by yacht is such a prize.

Once again the Walker family found themselves aboard *Aragunnu* with sails deeply reefed, thundering along, leaping off the occasional wave and landing with a jarring thump, making us wonder how it all holds together. Somehow it does and, despite day after rainy, cloudy day, with the magic of Radio Direction Finders, *Aragunnu* was off the entrance to the North Passage in the early daylight of New Year's Eve, the last day of 1987.

As usual, there was plenty of excitement on the way over but two highlights stand out. Late one windy, rough night, I was fiddling in the companionway with some shock cord when the door slammed on me. The catch hit my head. Almost immediately I could feel warm liquid pouring over my face. I felt my life force ebbing away as I dripped blood all over the cabin. My shirt was soaked as were my trousers. I bled over a sleeping son, Douglas, his pillow and the cabin sides. I pressed a towel against the wound and the bleeding stopped. I felt queasy, hot, cold and dizzy and thought I must surely lose control of my bodily functions. But mental control re-asserted itself, and I fingered a half-egg sized lump amongst sticky matted hair.

The next day dawned the same as the previous one – windy and wet. During the afternoon, a swallow flew close to the cockpit. This happened many times, then the bird flew into and around the cabin. The children were rapt but needed to be restrained from touching our little visitor. Eventually it alighted on the handrail, fluffed up its feathers and tucked its head under its wing. It left briefly when Cynthia lit the stove but returned for the remainder of the night. Comfortable on his perch, protected from the rain and wind, it seemed to recognise the security of *Aragunnu's* cabin. He left about 0730 next morning after sitting at a window looking out. Five little white deposits were left to remind us of his visit. What desperation must have been required to produce such trust?

Yet again, I entered the lagoon, having mislaid my page of calling instructions to the Harbour Master, who motored out to us looking a little peevish. He soon became his usual cheerful self when he recognised us from a previous visit. He told me later of a very real concern that the Island could be used for the entry of drugs to Australia so I resolved to make sure I followed procedure next time.

There are now new facilities for visiting yachts which are quite superb, having two toilets, two showers with hot and cold water and a general room, all clean and obviously well-maintained. I hope the irresponsible yahoos who seem to be appearing on yachts don't spoil things for others. The removal of the three moorings in Sylph's Hole was apparently due to a drunken orgy on a raft-up expressly forbidden by the Harbour Master, leaving the bottom littered with beer cans, as well as another yobbo who out-stayed his welcome there.

Sadly the yachts occupying the Dawson's Point moorings, other than our friends on *Realitas* and *Elke,* seemed to be populated by boozy foul-mouthed types. Drink as much as you can then have a good vomit seems to be the Australian way. Was I like that when I was nineteen? Helmut, the skipper of *Elke,* was met with abuse and obscenities on offering help when their drunkenness got them into difficulties, yet later he willingly went to their aid when requested. Has yachting become so commonplace that the camaraderie is forgotten? What would life be like without the older generation always there to lament over the younger one?

I visited Harry Woolnough, who is a friendly 83 year old. These days he looks after the Island's museum. He was unemployed during the Great Depression and sailed to Lord Howe in 1931, took the offer of a job, married an island girl and settled. Later he was employed by the Department of Civil Aviation looking after the flying boat moorings and other duties until retirement in 1974. He still maintains an interest in yachting and looks forward to his copies of the Coastal Cruising Club newsletters. He told me of his concern about the bureaucratic intrusion into Island affairs, especially some emanating from the World Heritage listing of the Island and the interference in land usage.

I suppose that like Suvorov Atoll, Lord Howe should have no-one living there at all but if that were the case, there are two possibilities: National Parks and Wildlife would prohibit anyone from ever going there, except N.P. & W. personnel or our Government would give a 100 year lease to the USA for a military/naval base euphemistically called a tracking station. That's more or less what happened to the island of St Kilda in the Hebrides off Scotland, once they got all the people off.

Fortunately for us, people do live there and I am sure they will do so for a long time to come.

Our New Year's Celebration was in a resort restaurant and was actually pretty awful with thick skinned tough duck and badly cooked vegetables, but it was with friends. Holidaying with our good friends from *Elke,* Helmut Pelzer, John Graf and Sandy Donaldson, and from *Realitas,* Ian, Jan, Jamie and David Mitchell, made for a wonderful few days. Sadly all good things come to an end.

The voyage home had all the elements of sailing. Beautiful breezes with the miles rolling off, followed by frustrating near calms and two days of only 60 miles, then strong winds of 35 to 40 knots to slap us around on the last night. Finally, we entered Sydney Harbour just two hours short of five days since leaving the Island.

All voyaging has its moments. It is amazing how the really bad bits are quickly forgotten when the firmness of land is underfoot. The time I think I like best is on night watch when the boat is sailing comfortably. Then I can allow my thoughts to take over. It could be *Zen and the Art of Sailing*. Interestingly Robert Persig, who wrote *Zen and the Art of Motorcycle Maintenance,* wrote a second book called *Lila* and the story takes place on a yacht.

Aragunnu leaving Lord Howe I. (Photo Jan Mitchell)

One sits alone, the sky thick with stars overhead, the boat steering itself and the mind free to watch or even direct the stream of consciousness whatever it may be. The thought content is forgotten but the time taken to while away the hours in reverie is not.

Mainsheet cover 1988

A Quiet little Cruise

The cost of getting the Walker family to EXPO in the school holidays of 1988 was beyond the family budget, so when we received an offer of a mooring at Clareville in Pittwater for a few weeks, no prompting was needed.

We invited Greg, Ann and Leigha Coonan to join us and made a day run to Maitland Bay, but heavy rain and head colds washed out the early part of our break. For the middle part, we decided to take a run up the Hawkesbury. We checked tides, dug out charts and invited Greg and Ann Coonan with daughter Leigha to join us.

Now you might be wondering how eight persons can fit aboard *Aragunnu*. It's a fat little boat with plenty of displacement for load carrying and has seven berths. The three Coonans moved into the forward stateroom. We stowed gear by the mountain and we pushed off.

We anchored off Dangar Island at 1800 after struggling against a fierce run-out tide backed by the river in flood. Only two miles were covered in the last hour with our mighty engine revving flat out. The next morning, we rounded Dangar and tried to rouse our friend John, but a new quieter muffler and eight lusty throats couldn't penetrate.

We tied alongside the wharf at Spencer for a late lunch. The river was up by a couple of feet and we had a battle with fast eddies and current. Locals at Spencer suggested we were wasting our time in struggling against it to go further up-river. The main flood was expected to run at eight or nine knots and hadn't reached us yet. Anchoring amongst all the debris coming down was dangerous so the upper Hawkesbury would have to wait for another day.

Back down we flew, carried by wind, tide and current. We tucked into a bay and with the anchor out and the stern tied to its little rickety jetty, we overnighted at Bar Island. We explored the deserted ruins and the little cemetery. At night we indulged in our Great Euchre Competition, boys against the girls. We'd played a lot of euchre on our South Pacific cruise but this time we had plenty of red and white wine and port.

On the Saturday, we motored up Berowra Creek. Unlike Cowan Creek it is relatively deserted, but there are a lot of waterfront houses on the western side as you get close to Berowra where the ferry is. We anchored in Joe Craft's Creek totally surrounded by bushland and unable to see the presence of anything human.

The next morning, on leaving, our motor boiled because of a broken fan belt. I tied the dinghy to the stern quarter and, with 2hp Suzuki buzzing like an angry mosquito, we were quickly on the move again whilst repairs were effected. Again we visited John on Dangar but this time enjoyed his hospitality. We took a stroll around the Island and met a long lost cousin of Greg's and got caught in a rain shower. Late in the afternoon, we headed down to Little Pittwater, anchoring just on dusk.

Next morning, we returned to Clareville but there were two brief moments of drama. The first was when we went aground off Avalon Sailing Club while off-loading all the Coonan's gear and the second was when we got back to the Coonan's house and realised Leigha was missing. Back at the Sailing Club, we found her playing in a rock pool.

We consumed just a little more distillate than wine and all ate far too much but it was just a quiet little cruise.

Gabo Island 1990

For *Aragunnu*, the 1990 Christmas Cruise was to be a voyage into nostalgia. Our sturdy vessel was built on the Far South Coast, named after a beach there and launched at Bermagui eight years ago. One of the aims of the voyage was to take her back to her place of birth, so to speak. We didn't expect anything mystical or magical to happen. The South Coast has called several times in the intervening years but each time, events have conspired to stop us. So it was a bit of Bermagui or bust (but more on that topic later).

Minor engine problems delayed us on our way down harbour on December 27th, but we were pleased to see some yacht masts at Jibbon Beach just on dusk. Not one belonged to any of our Club vessels that we'd arranged to meet there. A frantic check of the sailing calendar revealed us to be the only vessel in the right place at the appointed time. It seems that all the others had found the weather just a trifle wearying and a touch trying and pulled into Sydney Harbour to join the others for some essential R and R. I wondered if any were descendants of Drake, Rodney, Nelson or Beatty. They didn't tarry in port, drinking port. It seemed unlikely that any of our lot had any historic, nautical forebears. We joined the fleet as they swept past Port Hacking and no sooner were our sails filled and drawing when most of them signalled that they wanted to pull into Wollongong for a rest. It was lucky we weren't trying to defend our homeland from some invading Spanish Armada or French Squadron. Well, if you can't beat them, you should join them and so into Wollongong Harbour we followed for some socialising.

We experienced various adventures along the way, and when a southerly buster blew through, a midnight anchor dragging session at the Montague Roads anchorage in Jervis Bay, it added to the excitement of New Year's Eve. We'd only just got to bed and settled for the night. Fortunately no-one came to grief amongst all the anchor dragging. One or two exceptions, like those whose anchors were firmly buried in the weedy bottom, remained, and the rest of us motored the three hours or so down to the more sheltered southern end of Jervis Bay at the Darling Roads anchorage off Greenpatch.

Coastal Patrol Ulladulla provided showers at $1 per person and the pub at Ulladaulla provided Lyn, from *Jimbun*, and myself with some true blue Aussie beer swillers and some even bluer language while we waited to use the phone. The next morning, all on *Aragunnu* slept in and we awoke to find all of our fleet in motion. I think we may have set a record for a dead-to-the-world-asleep to awake-and-underway-out-of-the-harbour-start in just twelve minutes.

Finally, at Bateman's Bay on the morning of January 4th, *Jimbun* and *Aragunnu* severed the umbilical cord of the Club fleet and headed south for Bermagui.

Arriving there was a special moment for me. The narrow entrance was the same as always, although a little rougher than on January 24th, 1983 when *Aragunnu* last negotiated it. We stayed a couple of days, explored and caught up with old friends.

On Monday 7th, in company with *Jimbun,* we left for Eden. The air was now cooler and a welcome change from the oppressive heat of Bateman's Bay.

However the voyage from Bermagui onwards was dominated by a boil. The Walker family is no ordinary family, *Aragunnu* is no ordinary yacht, and as you might expect, this was no ordinary boil. For a start it was on Cynthia's bottom. Its excruciating presence made even a 40 knot gale pale to insignificance.

Aragunnu off Bermagui (Photo: Graham Solomon)

In my moments of despair before its true nature had been revealed I suspected that this thing, this emminence, was harbouring an alien lifeform seeking some refuge from a harsher place. But surely there are places with a better outlook? I gazed at the heavens and wondered whether Cynthia had been chosen as some 20th Century Christiana (from *A Pilgrim's Progress*) and this was her burden - which had slipped down somewhat. But, such thoughts had to be quickly discarded, when I realised that I am Cynthia's burden.

The further south we went, the larger it became. Cynthia's agony increased. Only by lying face down with the ugly protuberance uppermost could she obtain some relief.

Twofold Bay is worthy of a few days stay, although we weren't there long enough to do it justice. The Kiah River appears to be an interesting anchorage and East Boyd Bay was a delightful place to stop, overlooked by the mansion, Edrom Lodge, on the headland above.

Walker family in front of the shed where we built *Aragunnu*

Further south, we sought refuge from 25 knots of easterly in Bittangabee Creek. I explored the ruins there, as I had last done in 1977, but was disappointed to find a viewing platform and information signs firmly placing the ruins in the period 1830 to 1840 and so quashing the romantic notion that the Portuguese explorer Christavao de Mendonca had wintered there in 1523. One researcher claimed that the ruins were discovered by the Imlay Brothers who explored and settled the area. This researcher claimed that the Imlay Brothers had questioned local Aborigines who had told them the ruins had been there since before their grandfathers' time, which would place them well before Cook sailed up this part of the coast in 1770. Who knows?

After lunch, we pushed on past Green Cape and Cape Howe to Gabo Island, still in company with *Jimbun*. With good winds, the sailing was good but having many miles to travel, we switched on the engine when speed dropped below three and a half knots. We used more distillate than usual.

Gabo was the high spot of the cruise: from the restlessness of having wind gusts to 40 knots throughout the night in the little anchorage, to the natural wonder of the fairy penguins arriving each night to return to their nests. It was if a train had stopped just off the shore and disgorged a swarm of them. They arrived in a dense mass at the water's edge and started their waddling march up the beach, peeling off along various paths to their homes. Then a little later another mass would arrive seemingly all at once. We toured the lighthouse and signed the visitors' book. Fred Armstrong, the lighthouse keeper and his wife generously provided us with fresh veggies from their garden. We spent a few hours chatting with them.

The boil continued to grow. It appeared to be growing more the further south we went. Had we been going to Tasmania - I hesitate to think what might happen. "Let me introduce you to my wife Cynthia. She used to be a woman with a boil on her bum. Now she's just a boil." I knew we had to turn north. Graham and Lyn from *Jimbun* solicitously provided cushions for the wincing Cynthia whenever they were near and always offered rides in a slightly deflated soft rubber dinghy instead of having her ride in our hard dinghy.

Early on 11th January, we left Gabo for Eden. During a routine boil inspection, it burst. Without putting the readers off their food I will just say that Cynthia was also flooded with relief; relief from the pressure pain and relief that it was indeed a boil.

Sailing and motoring for 29 hours had us back in Jervis Bay where we rejoined *Jimbun,* our faithful and concerned companions, and met up with another Club vessel, *Realitas,* with the Mitchells and their two boys aboard. We had a lot to talk about, so socialised, swam and relaxed for the day.

Sunset at Montague Roads, Jervis Bay (Photo: Emile Jansen)

At 0645 the next morning we left on the last leg of our voyage. When I retrieved the trailing log impeller for the last time at Sydney Heads, the log read 503 miles. Our major cruise was over for another year. It had been a cruise of much variety: sailing in strong winds and light, anchors that held and didn't, lee shores and gales in the night, heat and cold, crystal clear water and great company (not to mention a boil on the bum!)

Grounding

The Royal Lifeboat Association of Great Britain provided a statistic that almost 50% of rescues could have been avoided if the people calling for aid had shown a little more self-reliance and a little more determination. A sailing boat calling for a tow because its motor has broken down, might be a bit much depending on the circumstances.

The late Eric Hiscock didn't believe in radio because he reasoned that if he got into difficulties he should get himself out and no-one else should be put in a situation where they were required to risk their own lives.

Running aground should be looked on as a challenge to overcome rather than a time to shout for help and throw in the towel. With that view I am loathe to ask for assistance. I have told myself that I would only take to the life raft when I could no longer stand on *Aragunnu*'s deck with my head above water. I would switch on the E.P.I.R.B. because, travelling with children, I recognise that they have had no say in whether they are there or not and I have no wish to jeopardise their safety through my own foolishness. I have never been in a life threatening situation, so I can't say whether I'd be up to it or totally immobilised by sheer funk.

Where there is not much chance of a life threatening situation arising, running aground is one of the interesting challenges a yachtsman has to face. It provides opportunities to experiment and practice what to do, so that one is better prepared if a really dangerous situation ever presents itself.

I've been aground quite a few times. The first occurred while ghosting up the Lane Cove River in our first yacht, a fin keeled Southerly 23. I noticed the dinghy overtake us. The soft mud was quite yielding, so with both of us on the side deck we reduced draft and drifted off. On the second occasion on the same vessel we were awakened by a strange sound. It was the keel scraping on the bottom. We had anchored too close in and the outgoing tide brought us to gently touch. The third time could have been a little more worrying. We were on a charter yacht and I didn't know where the deeper water was. Unwisely I tried to get off by raising the keel which only served to put us into shallower water.

When we were in the Gippsland Lakes there was very little tidal range and our difficulties were mounting. Before I had time to finish panicking and think it through, a small powerboat came to our rescue and towed us off. I should have left the keel down and rowed around in the dinghy with the mooring hook to find the deeper water, then put the anchor in the deeper water and pulled ourselves off after raising the keel.

The scariest encounter with the bottom was in a hundred knot southerly buster in Sydney Harbour between Cockatoo Island and Woolwich. The wind toppled a huge crane on Cockatoo Island. Our motor was useless against the power of the wind. There was zero visibility. I had visions of thousands of jagged bits of fibreglass strewn about the rocks of Woolwich. One of my crew stood in the cabin with quivering lips and trembling all over. Bob McNamara, the other crewmember, jumped ashore and went to phone the Water Police. They informed us that lives took precedence over property. The wind died as quickly as it came up and the bashing of hull on rocks ceased and I realised we were still afloat with no water rising over the cabin sole. I started the diesel and we simply motored off picking up Bob at the Margaret Street wharf. Again I'd called out before properly assessing the situation. Likewise, I was very unprepared. The anchor locker was padlocked and the key was on the engine keyring. Nowadays the anchor is always accessible.

At a bend in the Myall River below Tea Gardens, *Aragunnu* ran full onto a sandbank driven by wind and tide. We soon had the anchor out into deep water, but the falling tide soon had us over at an alarming angle. We would have to wait until 11pm for the tide to lift us off. A couple of power boats, seeing our situation, stopped and after much pulling and grunting we were off.

The next grounding was a little more serious. We'd sailed up from Sydney to Port Stephens and were heading up to Salamander Bay when I misjudged distance off and ran aground on a sandbank off Corlette at around 2130 hours. Very shortly after, our friends on *Sunflower* came along and, seeing our predicament, offered to help. I readily accepted as the solid breeze was blowing us further on and the wave action was causing some pounding on the hard sand. We launched our hard dinghy and Cynthia rowed a line across to them. They were maneuvering around and ran over the line wrapping it around their propeller. Now another vessel was disabled. Cynthia rowed back to me and I loaded the dinghy with anchor and a lot of cable which she speedily rowed out into deeper water. Meanwhile *Sunflower's* crew quickly got an anchor out so at least they didn't wash ashore. The line from our bow to their propeller was tight enough to play tunes on. It needed to be cut before the weight of our boat bent their prop shaft. *Sunflower's* crew pulled all the loose line aboard. We managed to pull our bow around with the small hand operated anchor winch and after a while found ourselves floating free. The Coastal Patrol towed *Sunflower* around to Salamander Bay. The next morning we dived down to unwrap the line and to find that, luckily, their prop shaft was undamaged.

The lesson was to make sure an anchor and lots of cable is instantly available. Having a hard dinghy helps too. It is better to rely on one's own resources. Having someone stand by is comforting but one should involve them only as a last resort.

Aground again

I must admit that I still regard going aground when no other danger is present as something of a challenge. The worst that can happen is that you'll lie stuck until the next tide lifts you off. An anchor laid well out in deep water and a dose of patience is all that's needed. Perhaps a little port or whisky, a good book or a hand of cards will help pass the time.

We had motored up the Lane Cove River – an area notorious for its shoals – to take a grandstand position watching our sons rowing in the Riverview Cup Regatta races. There were yachts anchored close ahead and a port hand marker on the edge of a mud bank. We lay to our 22lb Bruce anchor and astern, to hold us parallel to the channel, an 8 lb. Danforth pattern anchor on a light line. After a race or two, Cynthia noticed the other larger yachts nearby were solidly aground although on the other side of the mud bank. We would have to get out backwards and soon, as the water level on the marker post was dropping. I couldn't lay an anchor to our starboard beam as the Bruce anchor was buried somewhere ahead. Since the shallower water lay forward I figured the anchor might just drag through the mud if I winched it in. Hopefully the Danforth and the mud ahead would stop us being pulled forward. After a time and with some considerable effort on my part, I had a very muddy Bruce anchor and scope back on board.

Cynthia rowed out the retrieved Bruce anchor in the dinghy and dropped it into deep water. The decision to not try to turn the bow was made for three reasons: *Aragunnu* is fourteen feet along the base of its full keel and wouldn't pivot easily; it is impossible to get a good lead from the side to a conventional anchor winch (a vertical capstan winch would have been needed); and lastly a line out could possible interfere with the races passing close by off our starboard beam. We now had anchor warps coming back to each cockpit sheet winch. The 8 lb. anchor was the one needed to pull us out and was on a greater than 20:1 scope. Cynthia and Jane walked from side to side across the deck using their weight to set us rocking while I worked the winches.

The light line was tight enough to feel like a steel rod, but the little anchor still held. Slowly we edged our way backwards. We were becoming quite an attraction to the other boats whose crews were curious about our antics, although we failed to upstage the races. Those spectators probably thought it was to do with flag waving. Some eccentricity is tolerated in schoolboy boat races.

Eventually we floated free. With the races finished some of the boys came over in an outboard powered dinghy. We sent them in to retrieve our light anchor. This required a lot of tenacity and strength not to mention our shouted encouragement as it must have buried itself under three or four feet of cloying mud.

A later inspection of *Aragunnu's* keel revealed no trace of slime on either side of the keel to a depth of about eighteen inches.

Lessons learned:

(1) Rocking the boat is a good way to loosen the keel in soft mud, to cut a channel and to remove slime.

(2) Even tiny anchors can provide great holding power on a very long scope without chain.

(3) A depth sounder would be a nice addition, although I've always aspired to ocean sailing and viewed crawling up muddy creeks and rivers as best left to dinghies and other thin water craft.

(4) Engines tend to be not very useful when aground unless extremely powerful. An extra crewman may have assisted with the engine whilst I did the winching.

Naturally we were rather pleased with ourselves to get off on a falling tide without outside assistance and still make it to a sailaway in time for happy hour.

***

The river bar at Port Macquarie can be a bit tricky, and having crossed safely in *Revolution*, I was relaxing and not paying attention to the channel markers. Consequently, I missed the little dog-leg. This is right in the centre of the town with crowds of people lining the shore, walking, fishing, visiting cafes and so on. It was entertainment for the masses. Cynthia thought the best thing was to nonchalantly drop the anchor over the bow and shout back, "We'll be safe here." I suspect we didn't fool anyone. A powerboat offered to drag us off but our ten tons was in the tight grip of the soft mud. The tide lifted us off a few hours later. I guess I took more risks with Revolution than our other yachts because of its shallow draft and centreboard, so not surprisingly I put it on the bottom more often than any of the other boats we owned.

The Magician of the Swatchways
A Biography of Maurice Griffiths by Dick Durham

I've always been a huge fan of Maurice Griffiths (M.G.) and a number of his books are on the shelves of my library. He hated yacht racing and through his interest in sailing in the shallow waters of the Thames Estuary and East Coast of Great Britain, became one of the foremost experts on the design of shoal and shallow draft sailing vessels in the U.K.

Born in 1902, he had a remarkably long and full life. He died on the 11th October 1997. He was editor of the magazine *Yachting Monthly* from January 1927 until he retired in 1967. He designed some 140 boats and had well over 1000 examples built to his designs. He wrote nineteen books of which three were fictional, one dealt with the history of mine warfare, and the remaining fifteen were autobiographical anthologies of sailing stories or about yachts and their design.

Griffiths was awarded the George Cross for his work in bomb disposal during the Second World War, which he called "the Hitler affair". He rose to the rank of Lieutenant Commander in the Royal Naval Volunteer Reserve captaining a fleet of minesweeping and recovery vessels. He updated the Navy's Demolition Handbook and prepared the explosives in the ships which were sunk to form the Mulberry harbours on the French Coast during and after D Day. He served in the Suez Canal area and became the expert on shallow water mine defusing and demolition.

My hero didn't ever circumnavigate and sailed no further than Holland in the East, France in the South, Ireland in the West and Scotland in the North. He didn't care for ocean walloping or even for the Channel waters and the Solent. Yet, perhaps more than any other person, he was responsible for introducing yachting to ordinary people. Within a few years, after becoming Editor of *Yachting Monthly,* he had shifted its emphasis from South Coast racing in the big yachts and their attendant yachting fashions to "nothing over ten tons" and so set about convincing folk that they could afford to get afloat and enjoy sailing just as much as the snobs and members of the various 'Royal' clubs on the South Coast. He expanded the readership of *Yachting Monthly* from just a few thousand to tens of thousands.

After the war, when he returned to the editorial chair, he championed the home building of yachts using the new, miracle boat building material, marine plywood. He loved timber yachts, but approved of steel, GRP and if you could afford it, alloy. He demonstrated great tact as Editor, and the only absolute in his life was that he never used absolutes in discussing boats, be it rigs, construction or any other aspect. He encouraged any who inquired, but did not suffer fools.

Griffiths had a great sense of humour and was a fund of anecdotes and stories having a considerable knowledge of the sexual habits of people well-known in yachting circles. Unfortunately, none of these stories are in his biography or books, leaving such to the tabloid press. He was tactful to the last.

Although from a relatively poor background (his father was a womanising glove salesman, as was Samuel Goldwyn of Hollywood fame), he received a good education and excelled in English and History. He left school at sixteen and was mostly self-educated from there, driven by an inquisitive thirst for knowledge in his interests. He later became a Member of the Institute of Naval Architects.

Griffiths' first marriage was a failure and you get the impression that no matter how hard he tried, it could not be made to work. He was totally smitten by a pretty and physically attractive woman but, on his 90th birthday, he still rankled about the marriage failure. An inability to be able to reach back into the past and make corrections can cause frustration if it can't be philosophically accepted. It was ten years from the end of his first marriage to when he remarried and he felt confirmed in bachelorhood. By the time of his second marriage, he desperately wanted a wife who was also a sailing companion.

Dulcie Kennard, his first love, wrote under the pen name of Peter Gerard and was a fanatical sailor. To Maurice, she was his ideal partner. But her fanaticism was their undoing. Dulcie was a feminist who wore men's trousers, reefer jackets and had short cropped hair (as did a lot of movie stars a little after that time, e.g. Louise Brooks) and circa 1926, the movies only portrayed certain types of women by having them wear tweed suits with elbow patches, and sporting collars and ties. Marlene Dietrich, in the 1931 movie *Morocco*, shocked audiences when she appeared in a man's dress suit, top hat and white tie with a cigarette and monocle. Dulcie (aka Peter Gerard) had firm views and convictions. Whilst prepared to crew with Maurice, she also wanted to skipper her own boat. She hated the shallows of the East Coast, preferring the South Coast. She bought her vessel, *Juanita*, a ten ton engineless gaff yawl, and kept it until just before her death, never owning another boat. Contemporary accounts show that she was single-minded in the extreme, only ever talking about sailing. She didn't suffer fools and could swear and insult as well as the best of men, much to Maurice's embarrassment. He was always polite and even-handed with everyone. He was extremely conscious of his position and the need to never offend anyone. One can't help wondering whether this related to his awareness of the social classes in Great Britain and a very class conscious sport, in which he was involved.

Peter and Maurice were divorced in 1934 and she moved in with and later married Charles Pears, the Royal Artist who also owned a yacht and was an acquaintance of Maurice. Maurice felt relieved and conceded that Charles was better able to handle 'Peter' than he was.

In my library, I have a copy of an autobiography by Peter Gerard, *Who Hath Desired the Sea* and having read the book many years ago, was always intrigued with her life in that era when a few avant-garde women were starting to appear. In her book, Peter only referred to her first husband as

"Bungo" and it wasn't until I read Maurice Griffiths' book, *Swatchways and Little Ships*, that I became aware he was "Bungo".

MG's second wife, Coppie, came from a farming background, and he was able to introduce her to his form of sailing. She became much closer to the type of companion he desired.

Dick Durham's book reads like a Maurice Griffiths book, perhaps because it has so many quotes from MG's writings. It is an authorised biography but it seems to me that there is a problem with authorised biographies in that one is left with the impression that so much more could have been told. The photos and drawings throughout the book are excellent and reveal more when examined with a magnifying glass, such as the long sweep in the rigging on *Juanita*.

Just in case you are interested, there are long channels between the East Coast Sandbanks and just occasionally there are spots where one can sail across the sandbar in a very shallow draft vessel. These spots are called "swatchways".

THE COMMODORE'S DINNER IS COMING UP SOON (IT WILL BE IF HE EATS THAT LOT!!)

Iota

Simon Simpson was a public servant in the late 1960s. He wanted to cruise some of the world's more exotic locations but realised that he couldn't do it unless he left his job. The enmeshment that comes with superannuation, job security and so on made resigning an impossibility. Simon decided to build a "portable" yacht which he could send as deck cargo to wherever he wanted to cruise. His wife would travel with the yacht to supervise unloading and then Simon would take his long service leave and fly to wife and yacht ready to embark on the cruise. At the end of the cruise some reverse arrangement would be made. Because deck cargo is charged for block cubic volume, a yacht tends to be a very expensive item because of its appendages such as the keel and rudder increasing the block volume enormously. He chose a Waterwitch ketch designed by Maurice Griffiths. These are based on Thames barges having minimal deadrise to the hull, a vestigial keel and rely on leeboards to prevent sliding sideways in the ocean. Having a fairly blunt bow and stern as well as slab sides, it probably has a higher ratio internal volume to external block volume than any other sailing vessel.

In *Iota,* Simpson sailed to some quite diverse locations before swallowing the anchor. Simpson's wife, Jenifer, wrote *The Iota Story* available from Boat Books, Amazon, Booktopia and other outlets.

Navigation

Navigation was very different a few years back. You didn't switch on your chart plotter, wait for it to warm up, then be able to see your position on a coloured chart on a screen,

In the early 1980s the bang up-to-date whizzbang gear was Satellite Navigation known as SatNav. It was the forerunner of GPS, introduced later in the 1980s. European waters had Loran too but this wasn't available in Australia, nor was Decca, the World War II navigation system used on aircraft. SatNav was expensive and those who couldn't afford it had to rely on traditional methods and paper charts, which were still recommended even if you owned the electronic stuff.

One had to learn how to use a sextant and how to navigate with it. Proper metal sextants were expensive, but in the UK the East Berkshire Boat Company produced the Ebbco plastic sextant and the Davis company in the USA produced the Davis Mark XV. These were cheap and I had one of each.

Looking back, it seems like a contradiction to be penny pinching and own a yacht at the same time, however that's how it was then and to have one's hobby, one had to be economical within one's financial limits.

Coastal Navigation or pilotage is pretty simple stuff requiring just a hand bearing compass, a ship's compass, a knowledge of deviation and some charts. Celestial navigation is somewhat more complicated and in those days, based on the Marc St.Hillaire method.

Mary Blewitt was a famous British navigator who wrote a book on celestial navigation. Without going into too much detail, celestial navigation means solving problems in spherical trigonometry. Some of our older members may remember using trig tables in high school (BC - Before Calculators). It is a bit like that except more complicated. Before the Second World War, books of tables were produced to use for navigating aeroplanes, where the spherical equations were already calculated for you. These were the *Air Sight Reduction Tables* (I think HO 229) and I believe they had one volume for each ten degrees of latitude. Generally you should only need three or four (big, heavy) volumes. Mary Blewitt required owning these tables, so I had to put her book aside.

In the introduction to *Norie's Tables* there is set out Captain Ogura's method. Everything you need is in *Norie's Tables* (except the Nautical Almanac for each year) but the idea of wading through all the trig and Haversine tables to calculate a line of position (LOP) in the confines of a small yacht tossing on the ocean wave wasn't very appealing, especially when you had to do it again an hour or two later to get a fix. I did a course on navigation at the TAFE but still wasn't satisfied.

At the time, it was possible to have a dedicated handheld navigational calculator, I think made by Hewlett Packard. I believe Greg Coonan had one of these. I preferred not to rely on an electronic device and batteries.

Then I found what I had been looking for: *Self Contained Celestial Navigation with HO 208* by John S Letcher Junior.

This was a slim volume with the tables occupying 87 pages. HO 208 was the invention of Commander Dreisonstok of the US Navy before World War One. Using these tables required more entries than the *Air Sight Reduction Tables* but a lot less than Captain Ogura's method. So that was settled and it was just a matter of practising until it could be done with reasonable proficiency and accuracy. Letcher favoured a bubble sextant as used in aeroplanes and available from war surplus stores in the USA, but I already had my plastic items.

I tried shooting the early morning sun from the beach, but it was impossible to work out the height of the sextant above the surface of the sea as waves wash up the sand. So it was into the kitchen to steal a baking dish, which I filled with sump oil. Then it was just a matter of shooting the sun in the back garden. Eventually, I was producing LOPs passing through Gladesville where we lived.

To complete the navigation equipment, I bought a plotting chart on which to draw my LOPs, a parallel ruler for advancing the LOP across the chart, lots of paper charts of where we were going, and a Casio wrist watch, with known error. Of course, I had my trusty Walker Log for measuring distance travelled through the water. Thomas Walker and Co. of Birmingham had been making their logs at least since the days of the great clipper ships in the 1850s. I am probably distantly related as my Walker ancestors are the Staffordshire branch. Rubins at Artarmon used to sell spares for Walker logs. The line to the impeller had an attached weight and would wear out just before the weight. Some used to write that their impeller and weight had been bitten off by a big fish but I believe that is total rubbish and more due to a failure regularly to inspect the line for wear.

I also purchased a Nautical Almanac for 1986. Interestingly, Letcher's book has a perpetual almanac in it, but I was not able to work out how to use it

Amongst my equipment was a basic Radio Direction Finder. For this you need a list of places and their Morse code signals. I only remember Lord Howe Island as having "dit dah dit dit dit dit dit dit" (LH). Williamstown (for distance off) and Mascot (for direction) were useful signals to tune to when approaching the NSW coast around Sydney.

On the voyage to Tonga, I used only the sun, taking a mid-morning sight and an early afternoon sight to give intersecting LOPs and thus an afternoon fix. I reported our position to Penta Comstat each day during the afternoon sked on the Wagner HF Radio which I installed before we left. We'd sailed to Lord Howe Island in late 1985 and I did a course to obtain my radio operators licence in Radiotelephony (Restricted Operator's Certificate of Proficiency). I didn't use the noon sight method although I understand it is best to do a series of sights and plot them on a graph. I guess I just didn't get myself organised to do that. Cynthia, or our son Douglas, would record the time from the Casio wrist watch.

On our third voyage to Lord Howe Island in the late 1980s and the last time I navigated with a sextant, I was able to take upper limb moon sights as the moon was visible in the morning sky and thus a fix was fairly immediate. For the later voyages, I succumbed to a Sony Pixus and then a Garmin GPS.

AT THE ANNUAL GENERAL MEETING, THE RETURNING OFFICER ACCEPTED A NOMINATION FROM THE FLOOR

Self Steering

The most significant voyage of our sailing years was in mid-1986, departing from Sydney and sailing directly to Northern Tonga ending in Vava'u and taking twenty-six days. Our friends and fellow Coastal Cruising Club of Australia Members, the Coonans on *Nanook,* had set out a couple of months earlier and sailed via Lord Howe, Raoul Island in the Kermadecs, Tongatapou and the Haapai Group to Vava'U in northern Tonga. We left, planning on meeting in Fiji, but the Coonans were so taken with the Kingdom of Tonga, they suggested we change our destination. We were in regular HF radio contact and they waited for us in Tonga.

I had a small Autohelm tiller but the electrical requirements were far greater than our ability to generate electricity. Fitting out our vessel for the voyage had to be done quickly and not being blessed with deep pockets, Greg Coonan had suggested that we not waste money on expensive wind vane steering systems like an Aries, but look to a simple sheet-to-tiller system which he'd found in a book by Lee Woas called, *Self Steering Without a Windvane*. He had purchased his copy from *Boat Books* and he was using the system on *Nanook*. All that was required for our boat was an inner forestay on which to permanently set the storm jib, which would be used as a steering sail, some sheet leads and some lengths of surgical rubber. Even cheaper, I chose to use ordinary shock cord.

Woas' system worked brilliantly. I estimate that in the twenty six days that it took to get to Tonga, only about eight hours or less was hand steered. There were three times when the wind got up to something a bit fierce. The system still soldiered on with two deep reefs in the mainsail (no trysail) and just the storm jib forward of the mast, steering and sailing us. On one occasion, we sailed with just the storm jib steering and driving us along. Additional shock cords could be added or subtracted for heavier or lighter work. The failing of the system is that it doesn't work very well downwind, but I understand servo pendulums and the like aren't so good then either.

The idea that you can only do this sort of voyaging with a huge set of expensive junk hanging off the stern only goes to show how much yachting people are as much victims of fashion as everyone else. I suppose having all that on your stern shows to the world that you are a serious ocean voyager, like some kind of badge.

USES FOR A CAT ON A YACHT

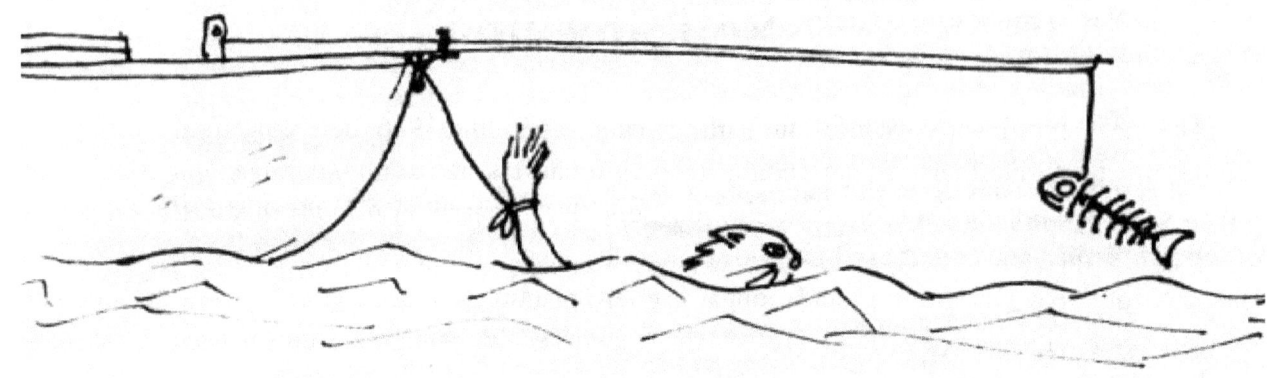

AUXILIARY PROPULSION (1 c.p.)
#6 IN A SERIES

Harry Pidgeon

I was intrigued by Harry Pidgeon after reading the all too brief chapter on him in Donald Holm's book *The Circumnavigators.* According to Nobby Clarke, in his book *The Evolution of The Single-hander,* Pidgeon was the second person to sail around the world alone (Joshua Slocum was the first). He was also the fifth person to sail around alone as well as the first to complete two circumnavigations. So much for the statistics,

Every Boat Show, I head for the Boat Books stand to check whether there are any bargains. Most recent years I have turned away disappointed. But in this particular year, lurking on the well-picked over central stand, I found a reprint of Harry Pidgeon's first book *Around The World Singlehanded – The Cruise of the Islander.* All mine for $10.

The *Islander* was a Seagoer design, being a larger version of the *Sea Bird* yawl designed for home construction by Thomas Fleming Day, the English born, editor of *The Rudder. The Rudder* magazine produced a book called *How to Build a Cruising Yawl* which contained instructions for building the Sea Bird and its sisters. It was of hard chine configuration. Day and two companions sailed the first Sea Bird across the Atlantic around 1907 to prove its seaworthiness and strength to readers of their magazine.

Some years back I found a Sea Bird yawl in Bermagui Harbour and, amazingly, a Seagoer yawl almost alongside.

Harry Pidgeon bought plans for the larger version and set about building it on the shores of Los Angeles Harbour in 1917. The Hollywood explosion was just up the road, but Pidgeon makes no mention of that or of the war taking place in Europe. He had supported himself as a professional photographer, taking, I think, mostly landscapes. Once afloat, he started making short cruises out to Catalina Island and around the channel between there and the Californian coast. This culminated in a cruise single-handed to Hawaii and back with one crewmember. In three years, he built up sufficient experience and confidence in himself and his boat to set out across the Pacific and maybe further. He sailed alone, because he found no-one to go with him. He would certainly have taken a companion if the right one had turned up. By South Africa, he resolved to complete the voyage alone.

Pidgeon was slight of build – what could be described as a 'spare man'. He was not a recluse, nor anti-social, but was independent and contented with his own company. In fact, "contentment" seems to describe everything about him. He was his own man. He was friendly enough and seems to have made many friends on his travels. He was interested in the world and its people. He took things as he found them. There is a sense in the pages of his book that he was well read and most likely self-educated. He writes in a simple and direct style which makes for easy reading. It gives a feeling that what he says are just honest observations.

Seabird Yawl in Bermagui Harbour

Many books of sailing adventures seem to over-dramatise and some authors, you intensely dislike because of their unbelievable stupidity and poor seamanship. That is, if they're telling a truth – perhaps adhering to the old adage of never letting the truth get in the way of a good story.

A voyage such as that of the *Islander,* took place in a time when the mere fact of the voyage was enough to excite interest and imagination. In that time the South Seas were still thought of as the province of Gauguin, Stevenson, Melville, the London Missionary Society and cannibal headhunters. It was around this time that authors Charles Nordhoff and James Norman Hall, both escapees from the rigours of the First World War and having moved to Tahiti around 1920, started to write travel articles about the South Seas. They helped to inspire people's imaginations, to hold visions of swaying palms, beside blindingly white sand surrounding coral lagoons, where white adventurers in topees romanced languid dusky topless maidens in grass skirts. There are a numbers of photos of this in Pidgeon's book. Both Hall and Nordhoff married Tahitian lasses.

Seagoer Yawl, Bermagui Harbour

Pidgeon's world of 1921 makes no mention of a world just starting to recover from that war. Ralph Stock, whose voyage in the *Dream Ship* was motivated by a desire to escape the aftermath of war, had passed through the Marquesas just before Pidgeon, as had Mulhauser. Pidgeon's book conveys a sense of freshness and wonderment yet one can feel a sadness and envy for those times lost in the past.

Looking at the little black and white photos of Pidgeon it's hard to imagine what he was really like. We have second hand accounts of many of the famous sailors but not much on the early ones.

With Pidgeon, we see an angular visage with hollow cheeks suggesting that he knew what it was like to go without food as a child. We see him smiling at the camera sitting in a Zulu powered rickshaw in Durban and another laughing pose with Alain Gerbault aboard the Dixon Kemp cutter, *Firecrest,* when the two great circumnavigators met. There is a more serious pose with Newspaper magnate E.W. Scripps. Here Pidgeon looks distinctly uncomfortable. Scripps was a man of wealth and influence and took a special interest in Pidgeon. Harry, being a typical everyman, may have felt blinded by the great man's light.

My favourite photo of him is the one in Holm's book showing a hatless Harry, by then on his second circumnavigation, filled out a bit, holding a halyard and leaning against the mast of *Islander.* He died in 1955 well into his eighties proving that for every year spent aboard a boat adds a year to your life.

Owning a Cruising Yacht

Aragunnu was built in splendid isolation. I had no contact with anyone else who was building a boat or for that matter even owned a boat. I solved innumerable problems as I went along and made a thousand compromises, some wrong, but there is often no correct answer. In the eleven years of ownership before she was sold, we sailed around twelve thousand miles. I learned a lot about myself and motivation.

Building a boat is a goal and you have to motivate yourself every single time you turn towards your project. Someone once told me that the desire to achieve your goal has to be like a fire burning in your belly. I don't remember that, but there has to be fierce determination.

Years ago I was working on board and a chap rowed over for a chat and asked to have a look around. Naturally I was happy to show off my pride and joy. We chatted for a while and he told me that I was the first person he'd ever met who had built a boat and was still married to his original wife. For many, the desire to build can be so strong that even the bonds of marriage can be broken. Of course, a man's or woman's dream to build a boat may not necessarily be the dream of their partner.

To own a boat is a goal and to go cruising is a goal. Many dream of going cruising but a dream is a goal taken seriously. The question is, what do people who achieve their dreams have in common?

William Albert Robinson circumnavigated in a yacht named *Svaap* in the early 1930s. He was university educated from a wealthy Connecticut background and, after returning from his cruise, he founded a ship building yard and built many ships and other vessels for the US Navy and others, making him a wealthy man. He returned to the South Seas after the Second War in a large yacht named *Varua*, designed by Howard Chappell. Robinson founded an elephantiasis research facility and helped to eliminate that disease in the Pacific. He settled on an atoll he bought near Tahiti, married, fathered children, wrote four books and presumably died there. In his book *Return to the Sea* (1972), he wrote, "It has been said that a man who has achieved all his dreams is the unhappiest man on earth. Perhaps I would be dangerously close to getting in that class but for the fact that for every goal attained, a new one has been waiting to take its place."

A goal has to be attainable. No good wanting to be an Olympic athlete at age fifty. For Robinson, the more unattainable the goal, the more ferociously he sought to achieve it. That's the way it is with many high achievers. The film star, Arnold Schwarzenegger, is a classic example. Goals need a time limit otherwise you can dream your life away. That's okay if you have no regrets.

Before you can think out a clear picture of your goal, you need to clear your mind. Your mind can be full of little critics that can tell you millions of reasons why that goal is not for you. Remember that critics have no real purpose - they don't produce anything and they are a major source of poor self-esteem, anxiety and depression. Have you ever seen a statue erected to a critic? The very worst place for a critic is in your own mind.

Some of the major blockages relate to financial security and stability for the children in their education and social life. Even fear itself. Life is full of risks and you just have to weigh up the probabilities. You can be unlucky, but some believe there is no such thing as luck and you make your own luck.

Once you have a clear goal, you need a plan: how long should it take and how will you get there? This is a step by step process which you flow into. Most goal oriented people make lists ticking off the items as they are reached. The tick is the reward and the self-recognition for each individual bit of achievement. It also charts the progress you are making towards the final goal.

The final step is the sometimes massive action to get it all underway. Hannibal set out from Carthage on three occasions to sack Rome. Twice he turned back. On the third attempt, after he landed he burnt his ships so there could be no turning back. Mind you, I'm not suggesting that if your goal is to go cruising, you burn down your house, but if cruising is not your partner's goal watch the matches.

Michael Jordan said, "I can accept failure but I can't accept not trying."

The last thing to consider is, will you be happy when you've achieved your goals. In 'Return to the Sea' Robinson wrote. "For all great goals are phantoms. When you are pursuing them, they are happiness. When you attain them, where are they?" Happiness is a frame of mind, a way of looking at things. It shouldn't be subject to another critic preventing you from enjoying things. One man said, "If I wake up in the morning, I'm happy."

Happiness can be so simple. Is there nothing better than lying in your bunk at night listening to the water lapping on your hull?

Step 1. Clear your mind

Step 2. Focus on a goal

Step 4. Make a plan

Step 5. Do it. If necessary take massive ferocious action.

The Last Hero

A Biography of Bill Tilman by Tim Madge

George Orwell wrote, "The year is 1910 or 1940, but it is all the same. You are at Greyfriars, a rosy cheeked boy of fourteen in posh, tailor-made clothes, sitting down to tea in your study in the Remove passage after an exciting game of football which was won by the odd goal in the last half-minute. There is a cosy fire in the study and the wind is whistling outside. The ivy clusters thickly around the old grey stones. The King is on his throne and the pound is worth a pound. Over in Europe the comic foreigners are jabbering and gesticulating but the grim grey battleships of the British Fleet are steaming up the Channel and at the outposts of the Empire the monocled Englishmen are holding the niggers at bay.... Everything is safe, solid and unquestionable. Everything will be the same for ever and ever."

Orwell was writing tongue in cheek, about the world of Harry Wharton, Billy Bunter and co. The Harry Whartons and Horatio Algers grew up to become the Sexton Blakes, Bulldog Drummonds, Richard Hannays and Biggles. These heroes would be engaged in derring-do actions and, even with a bullet or a splinter of shrapnel, would finish the task in hand before reporting for aid. Recuperation would be swift due to the hero's grim determination. He would make light of his injury and be itching to get back in the action of whacking the filthy boche, or whoever was the enemy, for the miseries they'd wreaked upon good honest folk. If our hero honoured a female it would be his sister named Marjorie or Adeline (never Susan or Helen) and if there was a love interest it would be his best friend's sister. There was no lust in these stories. She'd be on a pedestal. 'Jolly old Bertie's young sister, positively unthinkable old chap. Bertie and I were up at Eton together, (or) served in the Kings Own 24th Rifles, you know." There was no mention of bodily functions except for the odd bout of diarrhoea which was acceptable to lay the hero low. An iron constitution always brought our hero through uncountable hardships. Such was the stuff of fiction and 'The Boys Own Paper' lapped up by thousands of boys and girls throughout the British Empire.

In this era lived Major Harold William Tilman.

Bill Tilman was Biggles, and he was Bulldog Drummond, and he was Richard Hannay and all these heroes rolled into one. Just about everything written above did happen to Tilman and much more. He was indeed 'The Last Hero'.

Tilman was a rosy cheeked schoolboy at a Public School, who became a sixth form prefect, left to enter military college and was posted to France in 1916 as a Second Lieutenant in an artillery regiment before his eighteenth birthday. He rose to the rank of Lieutenant, was twice wounded and decorated with the Military Cross with Bar by War's end. He left the army aged 21 with enough adventure and hardship behind him to last a lifetime and that was only the first chapter in his astonishing and remarkable life.

Tilman spent fourteen years in East Africa carving a plantation out of the bush and growing coffee. He started mountain climbing there. He gave up Africa and began a long period of exploration and climbing in the Himalayas. With his long time climbing partner, Eric Shipton, whom he met in Africa, they became the founders of modern mountain climbing techniques. In 1936, he successfully climbed Nanda Devi, at that time, the highest mountain in the world conquered by man. Everest was attempted in 1938 after a reconnaissance expedition in 1935, and these two efforts laid the foundation for the successful attempt on Everest in 1953, and other high mountains. Sherpa Tensing Norgay was on both 1938 and 1953 expeditions.

Tilman rejoined the artillery at the outbreak of World War Two, was in the Dunkirk evacuations, and fought in North Africa rising to become second in command of his regiment. He became bored with this and avoided further promotion by retraining to work behind German lines blowing up trains and the like, and at that time, the oldest to do so. He worked firstly with the partisans in Albania against the Italians and then in Italy after the fall of Mussolini. Although a died-in-the-wool Tory, he favoured the communist led partisans as he considered them the best fighters. During all this excitement he managed to climb a few mountains in the Dolomites.

After the War, he returned to the Himalayas but realised that he was now too old to take on the very highest mountains over 20,000 feet. He became a consular official in Burma for a while but hated that, and at about age 55 bought a Bristol Channel pilot cutter named Mischief and became a sailor. For the remaining 24 years of his life he made twenty remarkable voyages to some of the remotest and largely unexplored areas in the high northern and southern latitudes in several pilot cutters, which he owned. His aim was to climb mountains that nobody else had climbed.

I suppose it would be hard not to do justice to the story of Bill Tilman. Tim Madge has written the story in a modern way with attempts to place Tilman in the context of his times and get under the skin of this extraordinary man. The man is a legend. He was human and fallible and he was honest and guileless. Perhaps as a consequence he made mistakes, especially in his judgement of people. When he gave his word he kept it and like Conrad's 'Lord Jim', would have preferred to die than go back on his word. Perhaps in his last voyage, he did just that. His trust of people was what we might regard as childlike and he expected the same of others but few could rise to his standards. Yet, he was seldom let down except on his last voyages. He was a small, slight, but wiry man with a wry sense of humour. He kept to himself and showed few public feelings, yet kept up an enormous correspondence with many people throughout his life. He valued friendships and had great affection for his sister and her family.

Tilman's death and loss at sea may be exactly as he would have wanted, although without the loss of the young men who perished with him. Such a man who was so strong and fit and had such endurance would have hated the physical deterioration he felt as he aged. His whole life was made up of challenges – the challenges of two world wars, the African bush, the mountains, the sea and the ice. He wasn't interested in glory. He loved exploring and winning through. He wrote eight books about his sailing adventures and seven books about his mountain climbing. I have read all the sailing books, which you can buy collected in one volume. It is wonderful reading with Tilman's humour creeping in.

Tim Madge's book is like one of those fabled journeys which, as it draws to a conclusion, you want it to go on. As I reached the last chapters I found myself postponing its finish. I felt sad that Tilman was no more. David Lewis told me he knew Tilman and had climbed mountains in Wales with him. A close friend in the Education Department had taught with a chap named Crick who had sailed with Tilman on the *Patanella* expedition to Heard Island in 1965, and told stories of that trip in the school staffroom. I would like to have been there.

We admire heroes, perhaps because they're people who do things we can't or won't do. We share their adventures vicariously through their writing, exercising our imaginations with word pictures, introducing us to people we'll never meet and taking us to places where we'll never go. Tilman packed so much into his life.

Harold William Tilman –
Born 14th February 1898 - Died 1977
(Photo Wiki Commons)

**May 1989
No. 214**

FINDING TREASURE ON THE COMMODORE'S TREASURE HUNT

Impressions of Turkey and the Greek Isles

Before the memories fade, I thought I'd put down some of my thoughts about our recent charter in the Dodecanese Islands in the Aegean Sea. [1992] The Mills and the Emerys were truly excellent cruising companions. Cynthia and I would travel anywhere with them.

In retrospect, we probably liked Turkey the most, but there were some notable drawbacks. Each day was like going out to battle knowing we had to face the touts and salesmen of Istanbul, who would be doing their best to sell us their wares. The most persuasive and persistent were carpet salesmen. They were also the best dressed, most well-mannered and probably the most educated. But sitting in a carpet shop drinking apple tea, chewing the fat and generally passing the time of day was just postponing the reality that we weren't buying carpets and ultimately we would have to deliver that message and cope with their disappointment. I guess they're used to it, but getting someone into their shop and befriending them is quite a good sales technique because it can be hard to say, "no" to friends. Coming back to our hotel after such forays, taking a shower was part of washing off what we'd had to go through outside, perhaps a bit like washing off the blood after battle.

For all that, the Turks are nice people. The men are rather courtly and formal in dress. They all wear "cekets" (pronounced 'jackets') in either leather or double breasted styles. The various vehicle drivers we travelled with showed a restraint and patience in the face of some fairly historic traffic jams. Perhaps it is the philosophic Muslim attitude of "so be it." Whatever it is, Sydney drivers sure could do with a dose of it.

The food in Turkey left something to be desired and may be the result of overlapping cultures leaving a product which satisfies neither culture nor palate. It was not *all* bad, but it would be fair to say that, in our experience, the Turk does not understand the concept of 'hot food'. I am referring to temperature not spice.

I felt some admiration for the Turk, perhaps because of the industrious attitude of a people trying to make something of themselves. Not that Bruce Walker could be said to be strongly imbued with the Anglo-Saxon work ethic. Perhaps I was drawn to the obvious pride that they have in themselves.

By way of contrast, the Greek seems to have a sort of pride in his country and we met quite a few who were very proud of having lived in Australia. It may be about flag waving and Greek possessions and the place of Greece at the forefront of the history of the civilized and intellectual world. The Greeks we met were a good bunch of people. The average Greek could be someone who just wants to be left alone to go about his business and sit under a shady tree with his bottle of retsina, plate of tomato salad, some fat juicy olives, a bit of fetta and gaze out over that blue Mediterranean sea and sky. His wants and his needs are simple and when you have that, what else do you need?

Turkish baclava is somewhat more liquid than the Greek variety but delicious nonetheless. Turkey is the home of Turkish Delight and there must be five thousand flavours to sample. I find it hard to resist and my increased waistline shows that my will-power is not up to scratch. We were tempted by a Turkish bath but lying there in all the steam, being massaged and so on just didn't seem to offer relaxation. The bath attendant in our hotel seemed a nice, gentle sort of chap, so who knows? I suspect that their baths are serious and formal affairs, mostly about getting clean and feeling refreshed, but we didn't find out.

Once upon a time, more than ten years ago, one could backpack through the Greek Islands on a little ship named the *Panormitis*. It would deliver its load to an island, collect those leaving and move on to the next island, returning a few days or weeks later. The tourists would stay at a pensione and tour the island by bicycle, moped, motor scooter or donkey. Two dollars bought more than you could eat and included the retsina. Breakfast was yogurt and honey, the sun shone down on the dazzling white buildings and the world was a good place. Under the trees was not only shady but felt cooler as well. The scenery hasn't changed all that much (except in the most touristy areas) and under the trees is still cooler and shady but those intervening years have made a mark. The *Panormitis,* having sunk in a storm, now lies at the bottom of the sea; it is no more and nor is that way of life. Tourists still backpack through the islands and ride noisy small motorbikes, stay at pensiones and at the many more hotels. There are just a lot more of them. The pace is dramatically faster. Huge liners disgorge tourists in their thousands and hoover them up again in a constant cycle. The tourist dollar now seems to rule in many places.

We stopped in at a very small island, Arki, which has a neat dog leg little harbour. This seemed an ideal off-the-beaten-track place with a small taverna and maybe no more than around thirty residents. Beautiful.

Retsina is a white wine aged in casks made of cypress pine. The pine resin permeates the wine giving it an unusual flavour. One of my guide books suggested that if you drink three of four bottles of it every day for three or four weeks, you MAY get to like it. In a restaurant in Rhodes we ordered a bottle of retsina to have with our lunch. The Greek waiter whom we had not suspected of being anything other than native Greek suddenly burst into the broadest of Australian accents: "Geez mate, don't drink that piss. It tastes like petrol."

I think it doesn't really taste all that much like petrol although perhaps there is a hint of petrol with a bit of kerosene and methylated spirits thrown in.

I wonder if we'll ever get to a stage where all countries revolve around tourism. Every country would have its own special brand of sightseeing. I hesitate to think what they'll use to attract tourists to Ethopia and Somalia. The UK is already well on the way with olde worlde shoppes, thatched cottages, the odd castle and *royalty*. People expect to see guards changing and trooping about as well as red double-decker buses and postboxes. New Zealand has dramatic untouched scenery, geysers, glaciers and big tattooed native people who jump around yelling about something and act fearsome. Australia has funny animals, scary snakes, sharks and crocodiles and a big rock. The USA has enormous vistas and lots of hamburger take-aways. The list goes on with some countries specialising in holy relics (at one time Europe had three hundred churches with Jesus Christ's foreskin amongst their holy relics) and famous battlefields littered with spent cartridges. The Greek Islands are filled with souvenir shops selling classical style vases with nude athletes on them, figurines, postcards and so on. In contrast, the shops of Turkey seem to have slightly more useful things like leather coats and carpets, and jewellery is everywhere.

The Greek Islands have all you could ever want to see of blue domed Orthodox Churches, monasteries and castles. The Greeks seem a little desensitised to all the history surrounding them and so much of their ancient heritage appears to have been preserved (and stolen) by others. Greece is changing and the value of that heritage and those remaining treasures are being jealously guarded. Some folk still seem to trash their environment and in places the olfactory senses are assaulted.

The Island of Simi was a particularly attractive place.

Cruising the islands in a yacht gives one a chance to get away from it all and find that secluded anchorage or the little deserted village after all the day-trippers have gone home. You can move away and find peace and solitude if you want. The cost of re-provisioning is heavy because the Greek hasn't really discovered the supermarket, although many small corner stores have that grand title plastered on the wall outside.

Rhodes, which I liked enormously, is the home of the beachside plastic sun lounge and plastic umbrella. From offshore they make a colourful sight along the waterfront in their neat lines of thousands. Under each lies a German, Austrian or Swiss carefully basting themselves with some form of suntan oil. Amongst all this are athletic young Greek Adonis types throwing balls to each other hoping to attract the attention of some tourist. I once read that the average time for the young single British female tourist to have her first sexual encounter after stepping off the plane in Greece or Italy was less than thirty minutes. Some mustn't have even left the airport! Just occasionally in Rhodes one sees lobster red English types strolling around, but tourists there seem to be mostly German.

Restored by the Italians, Rhodes has a magnificent castle and enclosed medieval town to explore. It was built by the Knights of St John who were forced to vacate, honourably of course, by the Ottoman Turks in 1522. The Knights were given Malta and fought their last great battle against the Turks in 1565. After their victory, carousing and decadence set in and they faded from history. Perhaps history will record our times as decadent too, but I'd like it to go on record that I missed out.

One thing that is cheap in Greece is Ouzo. It's not much dearer than wine and is probably not for all tastes but I'm partial to it. On unloading our rubbish from the yacht in Rhodes, where it was returned to the charter people, I was surprised at the number of empty spirits bottles. We had consumed a prodigious amount although I don't remember a single headache or a feeling of nausea. Steady relentless imbibing is the way to go, but going home to give my liver a rest was essential.

Some of my lasting memories would include walking around inside the caldera of the still active volcano on Niseros, meeting all the Greeks who had returned to Kaliminos from Australia, and the tiny Vathi harbour, Arki, Patmos and all the tourists. There was also the long night and anchor watch during a very fierce blow in Pedi Harbour on Simi, Kos with all its bougainvillea and crusader castle, not to mention the putrid sewage outlet in the main harbour. And memorable in Turkey were Istanbul and its covered market, Topkapi museum and Sancta Sophia, our night in an Istanbul nightclub and the belly dancers, crossing the Bosphorus, Gallipoli, Ephesis, and smelly Izmir. It was all wonderful.

USES FOR A CAT ON A YACHT

— WHEN SUPPLIES RUN LOW —

#2 IN A SERIES – THIS ENTRY FROM CYNTHIA WALKER

More Reminiscences of an Amateur Yacht Designer

Once upon a time, yacht designers concerned themselves with something called "hull balance", perhaps best described as freedom from all nasty tendencies when sailing. A yacht having a balanced hull was considered desirable. Yachts which were not balanced were "hard-mouthed" and difficult to steer with too much "lee helm" or "weather helm". A simple method to determine whether a hull might be balanced was to draw a graph of the difference between the immersed areas and the non-immersed areas of the hull sections when the yacht was heeled at say, thirty degrees. This was called Rayner's Curve and the symmetry of the curve showed how balanced the hull was.

Old time designers like Harrison-Butler and Albert Strange put a lot of emphasis on this. Harrison-Butler was an exponent of the 'metacentric shelf theory' of yacht design used to produce balanced hulls as close as possible to being vice free. The beauty of a balanced hull was that by adjusting the sails, the yacht could be made to sail itself without touching the tiller. This was much easier on a yacht with a long keel with the rudder on the aft end, or even a yacht with a longish fin keel and separate rudder.

When living at Bega and building my yacht around 1981, I was invited to crew aboard a Top Hat named *Topaz* sailing out of Bateman's Bay. I made three voyages on *Topaz,* once to Ulladulla, a second time to Bermagui and the third to Lord Howe Island. On a fourth voyage, which I was not onboard, *Topaz* ran aground outside a north coast barred entrance. Luckily it was scooped up by a huge sand mining earth mover and deposited in safe water and subsequently repaired. Being something of a know-all and smartarse, I delighted in demonstrating how easy it was to get the Top Hat to sail itself. All you had to do was to set the jib to be drawing properly on the course you wanted to be sailing and then adjust the mainsheet moving the main in and out until the vessel was happily sailing without anyone touching the helm. Dick, the skipper, seemed to really dislike this and usually rushed out and grabbed the tiller, concerned that something terrible was likely to happen.

Modern yachts designers adjust the lead of the centre of effort (CoE) of the sail area (area of mainsail plus 100% area of the fore-triangle) ahead of the centre of lateral resistance (CLR) of the underwater area of the hull to reduce the tendency of the hull to be constantly rounding up. At the design stage, it can be done with cutout bits of cardboard balanced on a pin head to find the CoE and CLR. The position of the mast is set to give a lead of CoE over CLR of perhaps 10% of the waterline length. If a yacht is hard mouthed and has too much weather helm and wants to round up all the time, then the simplest and easiest solution is to fit a bowsprit thus getting the centre of effort of the sail area further forward.

I guess it is all done with computers and CAD programs these days.

Barnacles on Propellors

Our run up to Lake Macquarie for the Easter break started with a slow run down harbour which I attributed to a foul propeller. I had cleaned it at Christmas but it was becoming steadily more sluggish. I attended to other problems and did not fancy a swim in the cold, murky shark-infested waters of the Parramatta River, so put it off with the vague intention of anchoring near Manly and cleaning the propeller there.

A smart breeze pushed us up to Terrigal and a somewhat weaker one took us to Norah Head just on daybreak. Under power and making less than three knots, we rounded Moon Islet to make our run into the Lake. Coastguard had advised that the bar was benign although a little choppy due to the run-out tide. Progress was very slow to the first port hand marker. Progress to the second marker was non-existent. Lining up marks showed us to be stationary. The hard running engine was starting to overheat. I suggested to Cynthia that she call Coastguard Swansea and tell them that a 'situation' was starting to develop. I was loathe to try a U-turn in the channel. Coastguard replied that they had observed our predicament and that Rescue 4 was on its way. By 1330 we were anchored below Swansea Bridge and had thanked Coastguard for the tow. We ordered a 1500 bridge opening, giving us enough time for propeller cleaning.

The water was chilly and very fast flowing. Fortunately our teenaged children were keen to do the diving - there are advantages to being infirm and having kids. I strung ropes out behind us and tethered Brian and Jane to us so they wouldn't be swept away by the tide. The two kids did the job effectively, clearing off a mass of barnacles.

We joined *Tahera* at Wangi around 1545 hours after briefly putting ourselves aground and backing out without drama.

Having barnacles on the propeller is an unusual experience for us. This had only happened once before and was, I believe, due to putting an anode on the prop shaft. After nine years, I noticed that there was minimal electrolytic corrosion around the tips of the propeller, which could have been caused by cavitation as much as anything. My view has always been that since they nailed sheets of copper on the hull of vessels to prevent barnacle growth for hundreds of years and since propellers are made of bronze (which is roughly 70% copper and 30% tin) they should be self-antifouling. My practice with *Aragunnu* was to polish the prop with a wire brush in an electric drill and not put anything else on it. I only experienced serious fouling when I used a shaft anode. Sometimes the prop had a little coral growth and could be slimy but had no barnacle infestation.

Copper is toxic to marine life as is modern antifouling paint which contains mostly copper. Two dissimilar metals when placed in a solute such as salt water form a galvanic battery which gives off an electric current. (Electrolysis not to be confused with galvanic action, is the process of transferring metal in a solute by applying an external electric current to anode and cathode.) The anode is the sacrificial thing which leaches out zinc instead of copper in the galvanic circuit when the two dissimilar metals are in contact. The zinc anode in protecting the copper prevents the copper from working as an antifouling agent. So putting an anode takes away the natural antifouling properties of the copper and it is likely that if you've coated your prop with antifouling paint its effectiveness will also be reduced.

So the possible solutions are:

1. Don't use an anode and don't antifoul your prop but expect that you may have to replace your prop every fifteen years or so.

2. Use an anode on the shaft and put up with barnacles, which is no real solution.

3. Use an anode on the shaft but coat your prop with an insulating paint such as an epoxy before antifouling it, making sure the antifoul goes on before the epoxy has fully cured as antifouling paint doesn't stick well to epoxy. Non-ablative and vinyl antifouling paints are recommended.

4. If you put an anode on the shaft, paint the prop with a primer before antifouling.

5. Don't put the anode on the shaft but put it on the hull nearby and antifoul the prop.

Lord Howe Island 1995

Introduction

It is true of life that one enjoys the hardest won treasures most. It is very likely that those who fly to Lord Howe Island could never experience the satisfaction levels of those who arrive under sail. What one must endure to get there stimulates the pleasure of being there. Imagining yourself in paradise you could actually forget that you were alive on earth when you are there except that there are usually enough little difficulties, like weather, sunburn or sore bottoms from bicycle seats to remind you that it is not a dream.

Cynthia writes:

Yes, we made it this time. What is it that keeps drawing yachties back to this island when it takes days of uncertain conditions and fatigue for boat and crew before it is reached? It is just the lure of saying you've been there and can receive a CCC of A plaque to show others of your achievement? I pondered over these thoughts as we left Sydney Heads at 2400 hours on Sunday 2nd January 1994.

I spent the first few hours stowing all our food provisions into as many nooks and crannies as I could. I was sure the boat was bigger when we went to Tonga. Our first trial came from our middle son Brian, aged 15, who had just completed an eight hour shift at MacDonald's before coming on board. When we left the heads we had a fair breeze but in no time we were left with slapping sails to rock the lucky crew members who had a bunk, off to sleep. Unfortunately this had the reverse effect on Brian, who insisted we turn the boat around and take him back to his own bed.

After a small screaming session with us telling him he was going to have fun on this trip and stressing that he was at least lucky to have a bed at sea. *Aragunnu* is certainly smaller with only three comfortable sea berths for ocean crossing. It couldn't be that the Walkers have all got bigger since Tonga!

We were not surprised when Bruce told us that only 70 miles had passed under our keel in our first 24 hours.

The dawning of our second morning saw us still with light westerly winds, so the boys put up our yellow spinnaker. Being experienced dinghy sailors, they knew that using a spinnaker was exactly what they needed. At last we were moving. For the next six hours our spirits soared and any feelings of seasickness on the part of Douglas and me vanished. The miles ticked quickly by and we looked forward to notifying our position to Penta Comstat that afternoon.

By mid-afternoon the boys called us on deck to bring in the spinnaker. The breeze was freshening. This was only short lived and the wind had soon dropped. Bruce was put to many tests when the weather became very fickle. We had almost no wind for a while then a very strong blow. The boat was hard to manage in the strong periods, and Bruce spent a lot of time reefing and unreefing the main. I lost count of the number of times he had to go on deck but as night fell we left the main reefed.

The westerlies were not to last and, for the next three days we had a north-easterly breeze. We hardened the sheets, *Aragunnu* leant over and we were off. Now normally this lean does not bother us much. This time however, it sat at 30 degrees most of the time occasionally heeling to 50 degrees. With so much heel, only two people were getting any sleep at all. I found it easier to do the night watch and curl up in the corner of the cockpit under the hard dodger.

The first night with the nor'easter saw white water running along the side decks. Hearing yells from below I looked in to see what seemed like a bucket of water coming through the centre hatch, landing on Bruce, sleeping bags and mattresses. Then came squeals from Brian as water started to pour in on him from goodness knows where. I decided to remain where I was for the remainder of the night. The next morning, Bruce made the discovery that the centre hatch had not been properly secured and sealed. He then went around with some magic goo sealing up all the spots that hadn't need it before.

Try as we did to dry some things, it soon became a matter of putting up with some of these wet conditions until the weather changed or we reached land. It was to be the latter. Bruce was running us in on the GPS which we were using for the first time. We also checked with the RDF. Lord Howe Island was 20 miles straight ahead.

This was not good. The northeasterly wind was still very strong and pushing us east seemingly for every mile of northerly progress. Having a very full mainsail on this trip, we reefed it to gain more of a northerly direction. I spent the next couple of hours scanning the horizon but seeing nothing. When the GPS indicated that we were five miles out, we tacked, running up the south-westerly side of the island. I did see a light off to our starboard a couple of times that night.

This tack was a pleasant relief after so many days heeling the other way. Just as the first light of dawn appeared, we tacked and headed for the northern passage through the coral reef. It was pure magic to see the dawn breaking and the sun coming up over the island. It was Saturday but when we called Clive Wilson he was already waiting for us. He directed us through the passage and up to a mooring near our friend, Hayden, aboard Wine Dark.

Hayden rowed over and welcomed us as he surveyed the havoc below. We put the mattresses out to dry and air, took covers off, washed down all interior surfaces with fresh water, cleaned and dried lockers, and collected washing and personal stuff for a shower ashore. I am being very sexist now. They are the things that I did. Jane and the boys swam off the boat not only to cool off but to look more presentable. Bruce and Hayden compared notes and concluded that it had been a hard passage. Bruce attended to our damaged foresail that threatened to get so tangled in its sheet that it might not have been able to be rolled in.

Which brings me to the question: Why do we do it?

For a couple of days before arriving, the kids had been talking non-stop about all the things they were going to do there. Now there was peace and cooperation aboard our boat. Being older, they were able to go exploring by themselves and make their own fun. Bruce and I also relaxed. Once *Tenancier* arrived on the Monday we all had many enjoyable meals ashore, the best being at Capella South Resort. This delightful spot lies at the foot of Mounts Gower and Lidgebird. The meals are large and delicious. It was important that it was for lunch because the dinners are much more expensive.

Only two dramas occurred whilst on the island. The first involved Jane. Somehow she caught the inner sole of her foot in the spokes of her bicycle. This necessitated two trips to the new hospital where she received excellent attention. Her swimming was curtailed for a couple of days. The other mishap occurred when the crews of *Aragunnu, Wine Dark* and *Tenancier* had arranged to go to a Fish Bake. As it happened, the crew of *Tenancier* were too tired as they had only arrived that morning. The wind had swung around to the south making the south-west facing lagoon rather windy. We still went but were very disappointed with the Fish Bake. When it was time to tackle the trip back, we decided that Bruce would go with Hayden in his somewhat smaller inflatable whilst I would go with the kids. Tactics should have been that we both hugged the shoreline until we were level with the yachts then head straight out. After going out a little way due to lines from shore to moored boats we just kept going. We were getting spray over us, but this was alright. It was only when we were nearing Rabbit Island that the situation became dangerous. Being far more exposed we started taking whole waves over the bow and stern of our inflatable dinghy. We kept going seeing the hulls of the yachts looming out of the pitch blackness. When Brian said he was losing steerageway I re-assessed our position. Instead of Rabbit Island being behind us on the starboard side it was now behind us and we seemed to be being swept out to the reef. We decided to head straight back for shore.

Using anything to bail out the water we rode the waves at a much better angle into shore. We knew that Bruce and Hayden had passed us as we heard their outboard motor and now saw *Aragunnu*'s masthead light on. I decided that Brian and Douglas should tackle the trip out again but at a much safer angle and without Jane and me weighing the dinghy down. I made a signal for Bruce that if he felt as I did that it wasn't safe in the dark to come back and get Jane and me, we would go around to Clive and Beth Wilson's place and seek help. It was with relief to see the signal, knowing the boys were safe and so Jane and I set off along the road looking thoroughly unpresentable, wet and bedraggled. Bruce had already called and when we arrived Beth was there to greet us. Not only did she provide us with beds for the night but we showered and rinsed out our wet things for the next morning. We also had a wonderful night's sleep and Beth fed us as well. The kindness and generosity shown to us was wonderful.

It was with much regret that we said our farewells to the Island and to the crews of *Wine Dark* and *Tenancier*. The skipper of Wine Dark was really looking much more relaxed and certainly living aboard was agreeing with him.

Balls Pyramid

Our intention on this trip was to do many of the things we hadn't managed to do before, the main one being to visit Balls Pyramid. We called Clive at 1100 hours to help us clear the island and within minutes he was beside us and guided us out through a passage near Rabbit Island. I gather that this was possible due to our shallow draft and to the fact that it was a very high tide. It saved us a lot of time as we put up the sails and turned towards Ball's Pyramid.

The rock is a spectactular sight with hundreds of birds swooping and flying all around. Each face had something different to offer us but we were, by this time, in the mood to be on our way.

We had completed our circumnavigation by 1600 hours and turned our boat towards Sydney. The wind was steady and blowing in from the north-east at 10 to 15 knots. This is usually ideal sailing and it was, in so far as it took us in the right direction and took us fast.

The only complaint was that we were now on a starboard tack and for this Aragunnu has only two comfortable sea berths. Our children are now too big to sleep end to end as they once did. Again I took up my night position in the cockpit. Bruce was wise to me and I found myself kicked below so that he could get a little sleep.

Each time we radioed in our position, we were delighted to know that *Aragunnu* was excelling herself with speed and distance. This was going to be a record run for us. The wind remained steady for days. On our last night we were tested again. The weather reports indicated a severe electrical storm coming up the NSW coast. The evening got darker and darker with mounting clouds. Flashes of lightning could be seen in the distance coming straight down out of clouds and hitting the horizon. The wind became lighter so Bruce decided to take down the sails and put on the engine so we could motor through the storm as quickly as possible.

I was steering, Douglas, fitted out in his wet weather gear was under the dodger, keeping me company. Brian was in a bunk sleeping whilst Bruce and Jane kept looking out, saying how terrible it was and quickly shutting the door before any rain came in. With lightning now coming every few minutes and hitting the water all around us, Douglas and I were wishing ourselves anywhere else but out there.

We called Bruce and asked if there was anything we should be doing to help prevent us being hit by lightning. Bruce brought out a short length of chain and asked Douglas to wrap it around the backstay and ladder. I have never seen Douglas move so fast. We then let down the ladder hoping that it provided a path to ground should the mast be struck by lightning. It's a scary thought knowing that you are the tallest thing for hundreds of square miles. With our precautions we only had to run out of the storm. This took two very long hours. A lot of the time the flashes of lightning were blinding us. Often, they seemed just a few boat lengths away.

As the sky got lighter, a gentle breeze rolled in. We called down below for the sails to be hoisted and Douglas went below for a much earned rest. But the storm hadn't finished with us yet. We had just passed through the eye of it. Being a touch frightened by myself, Bruce joined me so that he was just in time to be drenched with another rain squall. The lightning didn't last as long this time but we were soon reefing the main as the wind freshened.

As dawn broke we were only a short distance from Sydney Heads. We had made the entire trip from Lord Howe Island to Sydney on the one tack and so far it had taken a few hours short of four days. As I was coming out of my nightly stupor, I could hear Bruce talking to the boys and sounding very concerned. I was finally able to get myself on deck to see what the problem was. Our GPS was telling us that the Heads were directly in front of us nine miles distant. But we could see nothing on the horizon. The next couple of hours were very tiring; we were all straining our eyes to see anything that looked like land. It was unbelievable but our first sight of land came when we were less than three miles away. The smoke haze from the fires that had swept over Sydney whilst we were having fun on Lord Howe was still hanging around, severely reducing visibility.

As we entered the Heads we discussed the trip and all the ups and downs. The homeward passage had only taken a couple of hours over four days. The boys informed us that they were not yet finished with the island. This time they had made the hike to the top of Mount Gower and on their next visit they intend to do a diving course. I guess if that is the case, some of us will have to fly over to meet them or we will have to get a bigger boat.

Hard Dinghies

When *Aragunnu* was sold, the buyer, the late David Lewis, brought his shipwright friend Roger Powell to do the survey. Roger and I kept in touch, corresponding for a few years. I recall a letter from Roger telling me that he was flying to New Zealand to help Lewis sail his latest purchase back to Australia. Then I received another letter from Roger stating that he'd looked over the yacht, which was ferro-cement, and told Lewis that it was not safe and he would not be sailing back with him. Much later I read in Lewis' autobiography *Shapes on the Wind* that the mast on his ferro-cement yacht had ground a hole in the keel resulting in it sinking even before leaving New Zealand waters. Lewis and crew were rescued by helicopter.

Roger and I had some lengthy discussions on what constituted the perfect yacht tender. A year or so later Roger turned up at my house with a pram dinghy, which he had designed and built and which he claimed I had inspired. He insisted I have it. It was an early version and he later replaced it with an early production model. The dinghy could be had in nesting form or the less expensive non-nesting version. (I believe the original was given to David Lewis for his journey north on the H28 which he bought.

Roger called his business Fleetwood Dinghies and I wrote about it in The Mainsheet No.310. I understand the moulds were sold to David Bradburn at Lake Macquarie.

I still own this dinghy and it is a masterpiece of GRP design, construction and ideas. It is a nesting dinghy where the lightweight front section fits neatly in the more heavily constructed rear section. Its dimensions were set to allow it to fit in the back of a Holden Station wagon. Accessible buoyancy tanks are in bow and stern. The clever plywood central seat arrangement can be set athwartships or longitudinally allowing the rower to sit towards the bow when just two are aboard or more centrally when carrying three people. It has two rowlock positions. An aluminium strip along the keel protects the fibreglass when being dragged up ramps and there are chine protectors. Small ribs give foot purchase for the rower. Stainless clips locate and hold the two sections together and two 6mm bolts with wingnuts stop any movement. With a rear bridle it is easy to lift aboard with the main halliard. Of course it is wonderfully stable and rows beautifully.

I always worry that someone with an eye for such beauty and practicality will steal it so sadly it mostly just lives in my garden shed.

Fleetwood dinghy in nesting configuration

Fleetwood Dingy ready to go

A Revolution in the Coastal Cruising Club

Sunday 25th September, 1994 will be recorded in Walker Family History as the one day in recent memory when Bruce didn't own a yacht.

On Saturday 24th September possession of *Aragunnu* passed to Dr. David Lewis, author, Antarctic explorer and expedition leader, two time single-handed transatlantic racer and circumnavigator.

Aragunnu as sold to David Lewis – No dodger

On Sunday 25th, we drove to Tewantin, inland from Noosa, Queensland, and on Monday contracts were exchanged and *Revolution* became ours. *Revolution* is the original foam sandwich plug for the series of Revolution 38s. This one was displayed at the Sydney Boat Show in 1980. I still had the brochure. As designed, they were the late Ben Lexan's answer to the unstayed cat-ketch rigged Freedom 40 designed by Garry Hoyt in the U.S.A. The Freedom was marketed by pointing out that aeroplanes haven't used stays for sixty years and boats shouldn't either. What wasn't mentioned by the clever advertising executive who thought that up was that aeroplanes must undergo very frequent and stringent airframe inspections for stress cracking. Consequently *Revolution* lost its GRP foremast somewhere near Fremantle through fatigue. It was re-rigged using the aft mast in the appropriate place stepped on deck in a substantial tabernacle with massive stays and chain plates to hold it all up. The mast was a tapered GRP affair rather like a tree trunk and still a little whippy. To get sail area, a massive bowsprit and very long boom made from a large diameter carbon fibre spinnaker pole, were incorporated in the re-rig. The sails were made in Sydney.

The owners had been living aboard for some years, cruising the Queensland coast and ending eventually in the Tewantin marina on the Noosa River. They needed to move on. I suspect they owed money in marina fees. They said it was a "party boat". The vessel was fairly run down with a few things not working although fixable. Cynthia took to it right away.

The aim was to sail her down to Sydney for the October long weekend. For crew I had my old friend Greg Shaw, keen to do his first passage, and Andy Clarke who, coincidently, had been in Cynthia's last two years at high school. Andy had done quite a lot of dinghy and small keelboat racing and been around boats for most of his life, although with no offshore experience. Both proved to be superb crew.

We shared helming equally with Andy and I doing the deck work and radio operating, while Andy and Greg worked the galley. Greg did some electrical and engine maintenance work and I did the navigating.

We overnighted aboard in the marina and Cynthia left the next morning to return to Sydney by car. The owners had prepared the boat for us and we took around three hours to provision and fuel before heading downstream to cross the Noosa River Bar on the 12 o'clock high tide. Coastguard Noosa provided an escort as the bar is quite tricky being only a little wider than *Revolution's* length. The depth alarm sounded constantly as we left but we didn't touch. It was soon over and we were in the open ocean setting a course for Cape Moreton.

The GPS provided a constant plot and we passed outside of Moreton and the Stradbroke Islands during the night. By dawn we were off that stretch of coastline dominated by high rise towers and known as the Gold Coast. Just south of Tweed Heads we encountered a pod of whales. This was very special for me as I had never seen whales in the ocean before.

Off Cape Byron the winds increased rather fiercely. The sky was clear, glinting bright blue with sunshine. We took in all sail and switched on the engine. Not all the jib was able to be rolled up. I estimated the westerly winds off the land around three or so miles away at around 35 knots with gusts five or more knots higher. Not having a lot of fetch the waves weren't able to build up much. Under power we decided to head in closer to the coastline where we hoped the seas would be smoother.

With the wind so strong, it was difficult to control *Revolution* and the steering was hard, particularly when the wind caught the tiny bit of unfurled jib. Andy and Greg were resting below. I had been on the helm for about two hours when I noticed a square rigged sailing ship creeping on us. I was sure he could see us as there were people on deck. I called Andy up to have a look. As it came near a megaphone voice ordered us to turn on our VHF radio. I switched on Channel 16 and Byron Bay Coastguard gave me a lecture on not maintaining a listening watch. It seems someone on the beach at Byron Bay had reported us to the police as being in trouble. Sea Safety Canberra became involved and diverted the *One and All* to assist us.

The skipper of the *One And All* asked Byron Bay for a weather report and was told the forecast was for wind gusts to 35 knots, although they were recording winds much higher. The skipper of the *One And All* dryly suggested they call the Met Office and let them know he was recording gusts to seventy knots.

Shortly after, a wave caught us beam on and broke aboard washing Andy off his feet, filling the large cockpit with solid water and sweeping the lower main companionway washboard over the side. Water a foot deep was washing over the companionway sill down into the cabin. Being a centreboard yacht, *Revolution* has a relatively shallow bilge, so the cabin sole was well awash. As well, the bilge was full of distillate. I later found the diesel return hose to the tank from the fuel pump had disconnected. It was a mess. The spinning prop shaft and coupling was underwater and throwing water and fuel everywhere.

Revolution under sail in Sydney Harbour

We eventually managed to pump the water and fuel out and conditions lessened as we neared the coast and we motored for around 20 hours making only one to two knots and with fuel going straight to the bilge. We had used most of our 150 litres. We ducked into Coffs Harbour to re-fuel and Greg treated us to fish, chips and prawns.

From there the voyage proceeded well with sails up and speeds around six to seven knots, with occasional bursts to eight or nine knots. By two thirty on Friday morning we were plugging into a rising South Westerly about ten miles south-east of Port Stephens. The motor was on and sails furled. We decided to head back to Port Stephens to await better conditions. Suddenly the motor overheated. By dawn we tacked through the entrance and dropped anchor in Shoal Bay. The bubbling at the rear of the engine cylinder head suggested our engine had a blown head gasket. Andy and I made a trip ashore and bought some Barrs Leaks. The motor did not overheat again on the trip so perhaps the intake had been temporarily blocked. Some unidentified electrical fault had severely depleted the batteries and engine starting was impossible. Next morning, we called Coastal Patrol and requested a jump start.

Revolution on our recently vacated mooring, Bedlam Bay

After two hours and some reminders, the *Girralong* turned up. This huge vessel, manned by a lot of chaps, looks like a warship from the Second World War and is about sixty feet long. I expected to see a two pounder mounted on the foredeck. No wonder it took two hours. They were probably getting up steam and all just to bring us a 12 volt battery.

They were wonderfully helpful and courteous and we were soon underway. I was worried that the motor wouldn't start again as the starter motor didn't seem to be engaging. Northerly winds pushed us down to the harbour in fourteen hours and the engine did start and didn't overheat, so we didn't face a long tack up the harbour in the, by now, westerly winds. At 2:30 am, we were finally on my recently vacated mooring in Bedlam Bay.

It had been a rough trip and we were so tired that after a couple of Bourbons we fell into our bunks

One lesson learned is to keep the VHF on all the time at sea. Both Andy and Greg, who have their own businesses, brought mobile phones, which I think are also essential as back-up. Battery charging for them was through my inverter.

Revolution needs a lot of work and in my moments of darkest despair I would gladly have sold the boat back to her previous owners for ten thousand less than I paid for her. But, she is ours now and we have to get on with it.

Revolution awaits her new engine

Charles Herbert Lightoller

The young Charles entered the merchant marine as an apprentice at age thirteen, not wanting to work in the Lancashire Mills, where he lived.

Nicknamed "Lights," he was first shipwrecked by a storm on remote Ile Saint Paul Island in the southern Indian Ocean. He was rescued and taken to Adelaide. He had passed his second mate's exam but was serving as third mate aboard a four-masted barque when the cargo of coal spontaneously caught fire. He was promoted to second mate for his successful efforts in fighting the fire and saving the ship. By 1895 he had his first mate's ticket and switched to steamships. Twice he survived capsize, once off the Ivory Coast and another time on an expedition to the Klondike, where he joined the Yukon gold rush. Following his failure to find gold, he became a cowboy in Canada. Back in England, he worked on cattle boats and obtained his master's ticket. He served on various vessels and on a second trip to Sydney, he met returning Australian, Sylvia Wilson, whom he married in Sydney. She travelled back to the UK with him on the return voyage.

Lightoller's main claim to fame was that he was the highest ranking officer to survive the sinking of the *Titanic* and was portrayed by Kenneth More in the 1958 movie *A Night to Remember*. He was Second Officer and supervised the evacuation of women and children on the port side of the sinking ship. He dived overboard and was partially sucked down by the fast disappearing ship. He and around thirty others survived sitting on an overturned lifeboat. He was the last survivor taken aboard the *Carpathia* which came to the rescue. He wrote a book about the sinking and the subsequent enquiries. The *Titanic* disaster put a black mark over Lightoller's subsequent career, even though he defended the owners in the inquiries.

During the First World War, he joined the Royal Navy, commanding a destroyer which sank under him after colliding with a trawler. He was exonerated for this and given command of another ship which successfully depth charged, rammed and sank *UB 110*. The captain of the sunken U Boat later accused Lightoller of wartime atrocities for allowing his crew to machine gun the German U Boat survivors. Lightoller retired from the Navy in 1919 with the rank of Commander.

In 1929, he purchased the 58 foot motor cruiser initially ketch rigged and was to be called *Hobo* but the influence of his Australian wife caused the name to be changed to the Australian equivalent of 'hobo', *Sundowner*. During the 1930s, the Lightoller family cruised extensively, visiting Holland, Denmark, the Baltic and much of Northern France. In 1939, just before the outbreak of war, they surveyed an area of Dutch waters for British Intelligence.

In June 1940 Lightoller, with son Roger aboard, set out in *Sundowner* from Ramsgate to the beaches of Dunkirk to bring home some of the 350,000 troops stranded on the beaches there. Lightoller wrote, "We once had 21 people on board and I thought that somewhat of an achievement. Still I reckoned we might manage 50 or 75 and how many do you think we managed at a load? Exactly 130."

They survived bombing and machine gun strafing by Stuka dive bombers without taking a single hit by throwing the helm hard over at the last moment to spoil the pilot's aim each time a hostile plane lined them up for a run. They also managed to avoid having a stricken Junkers crash on top of them. Stirring stuff indeed, especially for a 66 year old man. It seems some of the soldiers were forced aboard *Sundowner* at gunpoint, after they'd heard who the skipper was.

Lightoller and his wife had five children and following the Second War he managed a small boatyard until his death at age 78 in December 1952.

Many actors have portrayed Lightoller in various movies, television series and documentaries. At age 80, Sylvia Lightoller led the 25th Anniversary Parade of Dunkirk Little Ships, steering *Sundowner* to Dunkirk. As of 2012, *Sundowner* is owned by the Steam Museum Trust of Kent and is one of the much treasured Dunkirk Little Ships.

Swansea Rescue

I dropped *Revolution's* mooring late on Sunday afternoon for us to set out on the first leg of a voyage to Brisbane. The wind was strong and gusty from the south. We fueled up from the self-service dock at D'Albora's in Rushcutters Bay and that was a little drama all on its own because of the strong wind. Cynthia was annoyed with herself about this and we decided to pick up our club's mooring in Vaucluse Bay and postpone our departure.

The southerly was still with us when we left at 0630 next morning. With fine breeze in the right direction, we pushed on all day, passing Sugarloaf during the night. The wind died off Cape Hawke so I switched on the engine and we continued, picking out Crowdy Head from the background of the Brothers Mountains. There was a strong smell of diesel emanating from the cabin, which didn't concern me until I remembered I had fixed the cause of a diesel smell last year. An engine inspection revealed a high pressure line to cylinder number four had cracked and diesel was spraying all over the engine. I wrapped a rag around it to stop the spraying and tried to call Coastal Patrol on the VHF. I could hear everyone quite distinctly but no-one could hear me.

Fortunately there were two factors in our favour. Our son, Douglas, had gone overseas and left us with his mobile phone and secondly, I had purchased Crawford's Book of Charts for Port Stephens to Bundaberg which had a list of all the local phone numbers of Coast Guard and Coastal Patrol. I did not require assistance as we are a sailing boat after all, but I was interested in what assistance might be available just in case. I spoke to Coastal Patrol at Old Bar and Forster Tuncurry and they informed me there was no assistance ahead and that Cape Hawke harbour was the better proposition.

The wind came in from the north-east at about five knots so we turned back to make for Cape Hawke harbour. I started the engine to give a little more speed and it boiled. I did my usual check of fan belts, hose clamps, water level and the like. I added some fresh water and started the engine again. Within two minutes it boiled again. The salt water coming through the heat exchanger was cold. I wondered whether the circulating impellor was damaged. That seemed unlikely.

We obtained a weather forecast from Coastal Patrol and were told the north-easterly was expected to last for two days. We informed them that we would return to Sydney. The wind held and we made good progress when just north of Norah Head, about nine miles off shore at 0730, the wind died and swung around to the south. The wind was light but the forecast suggested very strong southerlies with rain and building seas were coming our way. Beating to windward in big seas is *Revolution's* weakest point of sailing. Should we press on? With just the two of us aboard, we had been at sea now for three days and had hand steered for the whole time. The prospect of a twenty-five mile slow beat down to Broken Bay was daunting.

Revolution at speed

Our VHF was still not transmitting. We had no engine and whilst the conditions were not too bad we didn't know what conditions would be like in five or six hours.

It was time to act prudently. If we continued and got ourselves into some serious trouble we could endanger others trying to rescue us. If we sank, I wouldn't have to find a buyer for *Revolution,* but that was a silly thought. I called Coastal Patrol Lake Macquarie and told them I would be returning to the Lake but did not have an engine to cross the bar so requested a tow. Coastal Patrol called the Water Police boat, *Stackpoole,* to come down from Newcastle and meet us off Moon Islet at the entrance to the Lake. Two hours later after a fast sail in steadily rising winds, we met *Stackpoole* and had a heavy line passed over, which we attached to our bow bollard. The police ordered an immediate opening of Swansea Bridge and at 1045 left us tied to the little public jetty outside Coastal Patrol at Pelican in the Swansea Channel. There was a huge drama when a fellow, who obviously knew nothing about boats, tried to help by unhooking our bow line from the wharf leaving a screaming Cynthia holding ten tons of boat in a fast flowing stream.

The rain came down in torrents and the wind whistled around us, making me glad of my decision to turn back and seek assistance. I phoned a friend and he arrived next morning with gas bottles and silver solder to repair the cracked fuel line. When I had completed that job, we started the engine but it was boiling again within two minutes. We agreed that we had a blown head gasket with exhaust gas blowing into the water galleries, and just possibly a cracked cylinder head.

My friend drove me back to Sydney and I hoped to get things sorted before Easter shut everything down, but the engineering company in West Ryde, who were engaged to true up the cylinder head, would not do anything before the following Tuesday. Getting to Queensland was becoming more remote.

Easter was a misery, with four days of beating rain and heavy winds. Because we were nearly beam on, rain blew in everywhere despite our awning. Peevish fishermen asked us how long we expected to be on the wharf. With no sun for the solar panels, our batteries started to run down. I'd brought a charger up from Sydney and began a daily ritual of battery charging. The Coast Patrol people whose wharf we were occupying were wonderfully helpful and patient, providing hot showers and toilets.

The engineering company in West Ryde skimmed the Mercedes OM 636 cylinder head on the Tuesday and I bought new cylinder head bolts. I also ordered a new head gasket to be made by Swanson's at Asquith. On the Wednesday, I carefully reassembled it all, tensioning the head bolts with a tension wrench, but the batteries did not seem to have enough charge for starting. We left the batteries on charge and drove back to Sydney returning the next morning. Even with fully charged batteries, the motor could barely turn over. In a moment of pure inspiration I phoned a marine electrician friend, named Lloyd Hammond. He told me that not enough current was getting through because the cap over the brushes was mostly likely filled with grease and gunk, causing the brushes to stick in their holders. Lloyd is a genius.

I cleaned out a couple of spoonsful of grease and carbon dust and wire brushed the black commutator back to a nice brass colour and reassembled it all. The motor roared to life, but our troubles were not over yet. The hand of fate that controls these things had a couple of more swipes in store for us.

About this time I discovered a timber lining I had installed behind the chart table had crushed the coaxial VHF aerial cable. I don't know whether coaxial cable is like water hose in that if you crush it, less gets through. But the more likely cause was that the contacts in the fuse holder were making poor contact. After a rub with emery paper, our VHF was back to normal for transmitting.

We ordered a three o'clock bridge opening and were told the bridge hydraulics were playing up and the operator didn't want any delays. We pushed hard against the incoming tide and with perfect timing and judgement, Cynthia had *Revolution* only half a boat length away when the now open bridge light turned to green.

The forecast was for light southerlies so we decided to motor sail all the way back if necessary, using the autopilot. After a few miles, I became aware that we had no steering. The hydraulic reservoir had run low, so it was out with the spanners again. Not long after, Cynthia noticed the engine temperature rising. With a despairing sigh I climbed back down into the engine bay with a torch to see if I could spot anything obvious. I noticed one of the large jubilee clamps on the heat exchanger had broken and water was leaking out. My earlier checks had not revealed any water escaping.

Finally on Friday we picked up our mooring in Sydney. A few days of leave and our holiday had slipped by. What a holiday!

Sculling

I'd read an article about sculling and decided to give it a go. Knowing what you are doing and practice appeared to be all there was to it. It was an easy job to cut a notch in the transom of my wooden dinghy. I came to regard the presence of a sculling notch in the stern of a hard dinghy as the mark of a consummate yachtsman.

To scull, basically you twist the oar and move it from side to side in a saw tooth pattern. If you are doing it properly the oar is pressing against the hull and moving it forward. Steering is easy as you give more weight to one side or the other. Experienced scullers can move quite heavy vessels. I remember seeing a photo of the late Eric Tabarley sculling quite a large workboat. The Chinese have a long curved sweep called a "yuloh," which has a line under the handle attached to a thwart. The line serves to twist the sweep so that the operator only has to move it from side to side. These sweeps have been around for hundreds of years.

After a bit of practice, I could get into the rhythm of the thing and send the dinghy forward at a reasonable speed, in any direction I wanted. It was a new skill.

Dick Keyes was a CCCA member who owned a PR25 yacht *Snagg L Too.* Dick had served in the US Army in Korea post Korean War and pre Vietnam War and had washed ashore in Australia at some stage, marrying Keitha and settling down with their son in Sydney. I once crewed with Dick on a trip from Lake Macquarie to Broken Bay.

Dick occasionally singled-handed and, on one sailaway, was anchored in Americas Bay not too far from us. It was dark and I decided to join him on his yacht, sculling over. Confident of my sculling, I had left the other oar on our yacht, *Aragunnu.* When it came time to return the wind was up somewhat and seriously whistling down the Bay. It was upwind to return. My sculling just wasn't good enough to make progress and I found myself being blown towards Refuge Bay and possibly out into Cowan Creek. Fortunately I reached over and grabbed a mooring as I was being whisked past. I sat huddled there for about half an hour until the wind eased and was then able to make it back to our own boat.

I don't remember doing much sculling after that.

On Communications in the 1990s

I received an email from friends advising me that they now had an e-mail address. It started me thinking – always a dangerous sign.

We have become obsessed with letting people know where we are. A mobile phone is now the mandatory fashion accessory of the young and just about everyone else. No businessman can live without one. It started with answering machines, where you could make contact even if the person was unavailable. Then we got call-waiting, so if someone is ringing through you don't have to miss their call if you're speaking to someone else. Now we have e-mail, where you can get messages through your computer and it is amazing what you can get through your computer these days. All newly born and existing cats and dogs have to have implanted silicon chips since July 1998 so we know whom they belong to and maybe even knowing where they are. How long before we have to have implanted silicon chips?

Imagine this conversation:

"Has your baby had his chip in yet?"

"No, dear, we're waiting until he/she turns one before we have him/her done but we'll be having a Chip Implant Party when we do. We've already got him his first cellular phone. You know, the one that translates baby talk. Mind you, in our day we didn't have to get our chips in until we were three."

Suddenly, we have to know where everyone is. The phone rings. It's just someone letting you know where they are. I suspect it's all a great marketing ploy to make us feel guilty and uncaring. If you don't know where Fred is, you're a louse. They ran a series of advertisements encouraging people to ring home to the UK, Italy, Greece or wherever and how excited the folks there will be to hear from you. I felt so left out. I wanted to arrange surrogate rellies in Europe so I could call and tell them how I was and indeed where I was. As always, the aim in all of this is to make money and lots of it, and it's been hugely successful. It wouldn't be fair to have governments make all that money so the telephone corporations were privatised.

In the old days if someone didn't answer their phone, they weren't home or it was engaged - no cost to either party. If it was important, you rang them back at a cost of one phone call. Nowadays you leave a message (cost to you - one call) then they call you back (cost to them - one call) but you're on the line and luckily you have call-waiting, you can tell them you'll call them back (cost to you - one call). The end result is that three calls have been made for one conversation. You can see who benefits. They give away mobile phones to get you signed up for all those calls and services and message bank. We are told that mobile phone calls are only charged for on the time they take. Does anyone measure how long their calls are?

Psychologically you've been manipulated into feeling guilty if you don't stay in touch and you'll find yourself worrying if someone doesn't call you.

I'm standing up to say I don't want to be found. I don't care where you are. I trust that you are big enough and intelligent enough to look after yourself and stand on your own two feet and that you are enjoying yourself wherever you are. If you aren't, then, that's your problem.

When I'm on my boat, I don't turn on my VHF unless I want to make a call or hear the weather. I don't want to listen to all the inane calls of people telling each other where they are. I carry an EPIRB and a marine radio as required by law but it does place me into a hypocritical position and I guess my position can be seen as selfish. I am prepared to go to the rescue of others should I see a distress flare or vessel on fire, aground or whatever. There is a responsibility for the captain of a vessel to ensure the safety of his crew and a person also has a responsibility to one's dependents which I am keenly aware of. Although never faced with any really dangerous situations I hope that I would be able to give my life to save others if called upon. Lucky for me that resolve hasn't been tested.

It may be that the communications industry has blurred the line between what is useful or essential knowledge and what is dross. I hope I'm still able to tell the difference.

Some More Reminiscences

David Lewis bought *Aragunnu* and renamed it *Southern Seas II*. He was 78 years of age and was working as a medical locum.

He paid me with a bundle of cheques signed by different people and off he went, taking *Southern Seas II* to Lake Macquarie where he did some work to make it more to his liking. Then he set off for the Pacific. He visited Samoa and met up with some of his old associates who had taught him Polynesian navigation methods. He wrote to me praising the yacht's stability and safety in some very heavy weather north of New Zealand in which another yacht was lost.

On one voyage, he had aboard a film crew making a documentary about him. I believe it was for SBS but I don't think it has ever been aired. Of course, I'd have loved to see it.

David Lewis on *Southern Seas II in Samoa*
He collected and re-attached the fibreglass dodger. (Photo: David Hoyle)

Lewis eventually returned to New Zealand and being a New Zealand icon, was tied up to the Maritime Museum wharf in the centre of Auckland. He wanted to sail to Spain and felt *Southern Seas II* too slow to ever get there, so he sold it and bought a much bigger ferro-cement vessel. The yacht he'd arrived in to Australia before buying *Southern Seas II* belonged to his lady partner and was also ferro-cement, so I guess he had a liking for the material.

Southern Seas II in Samoa (Photo: David Hoyle)

Southern Seas II was sold yet again and sailed back to Australia by its new owner eventually ending up in Tasmania, where the owner took out the Dong Feng engine and put in something less troublesome, a Lister 18 hp unit. There is another story in that as well. In a fairly run-down state, the vessel was taken to Kettering where a complete refurbishment took place over a three and a half year period. Very smart she looked, too. An article about her history and relaunching appeared in the Hobart Mercury dated March 29th 2003. I was able to see her on a mooring at Kettering and take some photos.

I understand *Aragunnu/Southern Seas II* was sold yet again and was relocated to Cygnet where she remains to this day.

Every two years when I go down to Tasmania for the Wooden Boat Festival, I drive down to Cygnet and gaze out with my binoculars. The mooring is a long way from the shore.

I like to think that perhaps there are still great voyages ahead for my old yacht.

Southern Seas II undergoing restoration in Kettering

Southern Seas II after restoration, Kettering

Arthur Ransome

I became an instant Ransome fan when I read the opening lines of his book *Racundra's First Cruise:* "Houses are but badly built boats so firmly aground that you cannot think of moving them. They are definitely inferior things... the desire to build a house is the tired wish of a man content thenceforward with a single anchorage. The desire to build a boat is the desire of youth unwilling yet to accept the idea of a final resting place."

Ransome eventually sets sail on *Racundra* with his crew, the Ancient Mariner and the Cook, who he does not identify as his mistress Evgenia, due to his still being married to one Ivy Walker (not related to me as far as I know), from whom he escaped by moving to Russia. Once divorced from Ivy, he married Evgenia in 1924. *Racundra* was later sold to Adlard Coles and renamed *Anntte II*. Coles, an accountant, was inspired to write his great work, *Heavy Weather Sailing*, after encountering a storm in the North Sea aboard *Racundra*. Perhaps because he had trouble finding a publisher, Coles founded the publishing house in his name specialising in nautical books. Coles' autobiography, *The Sailing Years,* is a good read.

In 1914, Ransome went to Russia to become the news correspondent for *The Daily News* and from 1919, Special Correspondent for *The Manchester Guardian.* This was the period of the First World War and the Russian Revolution. It was most likely quite exciting, although perhaps not so much at the time, with dangers on all sides. Ransome talked his way out of some close scrapes with both the White and Red armies (such as being summarily shot). Some have speculated that he was spying for the British Government, others that he was a communist sympathiser. He certainly met Lenin and a host of others. Ransome had a manner which people liked and he made friends easily. Evgenia Petrovna Shelepina, who became his mistress and later wife, was Trotsky's secretary. After the War, they settled in Tallinn, Estonia, where they did some sailing in their first boats. They moved to Riga in Latvia in late 1921 and had *Racundra* built there.

The Ransomes moved to the Lakes District in late 1924. He resigned from the newspaper and from 1930 to 1943 wrote a *Swallows and Amazons* book each year except for 1942. Ransome was a keen fisherman and enjoyed catching eels from a number of hire yachts and power boats on the Norfolk Broads.

He moved to the east coast, settling near Pin Mill and bought a yacht which he named *Nancy Blackett*. This became the *Goblin* in his book, *We Didn't Mean to go to Sea*. At Harry King's yard at Pin Mill, he had *Selina King* built, which I regard as his prettiest yacht. The ever restless Ransome had *Peter Duck*, a Laurent Giles designed ketch, built in 1946 and then in 1952, bought *Lottie Blossom,* a Hilliard built 27' centre cockpit double-ender. Less than one season later and, still not satisfied, he commissioned *Lottie Blossom* II in 1953, another 27' Hilliard except with an aft cockpit. This was his last vessel and he cruised all over the south coast and across to France while he was able. All his vessels, from *Selina King* onwards, seemed to have been plagued with problems. He swallowed the anchor in the late 1950s. Each of his yachts have been located and restored, including the dinghy, *Mavis*. The dinghy, *Swallow,* is lost. His final two books about fishing were published around that time.

The Ransome Society is a very active organisation with branches in countries like Japan. He has achieved 'cult status' and everything he ever did, thought, said or wrote is studied and regarded with mystical reverence by his followers.

Roger Wardell is one such devotee and wrote *Nancy Blackett - Under Sail with Arthur Ransome,* as a celebration of Ransome's life, as much as a biography. Ransome himself wrote an autobiography which only covered the years to 1932.

Ransome's fame comes from his series of children's book starting with *Swallows and Amazons,* which I must confess, I haven't read, nor any of the others. Ransome's father, Professor Cyril Ransome, had corresponded with W.G. Collingwood from 1885 and when Arthur met W.G. on a holiday to the Lakes District in 1904 it bordered on a religious experience for young Arthur, so enraptured was he by Collingwood's fame in literary and artistic circles.

The slightly Bohemian Collingwoods, Gershom (W.G.) and Edith (Dorrie) were both writers and artists and moved to a cottage on the shore of Lake Windemere, later moving to Lanehead, on the shore of Coniston Water, after the birth of their four children: Dora, Barbara, Robin and Ursula. Gershom wrote *The Life and Work of John Ruskin* about his great friend and mentor.

It was into this family that Arthur Ransom was invited. Ransome's decision to become a poet and writer, although accepted by his mother, was a change of direction for members of the Ransome family, whose vocation lay in the sciences. Ransome must have felt totally accepted when W.G. made it clear that aspiring to be a poet was a perfectly acceptable thing to be. The Collingwood house, where Ransome stayed, was filled with books from floor to ceiling, and art works. Robin Collingwood was away at university at that time so Ransome slept in his bed. Edith would rouse the family each morning with piano recitals of Beethoven, then there was writing until lunch and into the afternoon, followed by reading in the garden, posing for portraits or going for sailing trips to Peel Island for picnics or camping. He became quickly accepted as an adopted relative. He called Edith Collingwood "Aunt". He proposed to Dora often. She wrote, "He seems to want to marry anyone and everyone - anything for a wife." Ransome actually proposed to just about every female of his acquaintance, which became a standing joke amongst his friends.

Back in London, Arthur Ransome was becoming a successful writer and had moved to Chelsea and was associating with the Chestertons, Bram Stoker and W.B. Yeats. He loved the whole bohemian scene of literary London and perhaps it was the golden age for him.

No-one was more astonished than Ransome himself when one Ivy Constance Walker accepted his marriage proposal in 1909. Ivy seemed a rather complex person, snobbish, melodramatic, jealous, and a spendthrift with an insatiable hunger for attention. Predictably, she didn't like the Collingwoods. On the plus side, Ivy was a good writer, who helped Arthur with his research, ran his household and admired him intensely. But Ivy's mother seems to have been quite 'nutty'. She was a constant interference in the marriage.

The conflicts in the marriage became too much for the affable Ransome, who was trying hard to focus on his literary career. He found it very difficult to break away from Ivy and seemed to always choose the non-confrontational escape path by running away, which he finally did in 1914.

Robin Collingwood and Ernest Altounyan were at Rugby School together and became firm friends. Ernest too was drawn to the eccentric atmosphere of the Collingwood household and, like Ransome, felt he belonged there. Ernest and Arthur Ransome competed for the affections of Robin's sisters, the Collingwood girls.

The oldest Collingwood daughter married Ernest Altounyan, who was half Irish, half Armenian, a doctor and keen sailor. After his medical graduation and service in World War One, the Altounyans moved to Aleppo in Syria where Ernest worked in his father's hospital. They returned to the grandparents' house in the Lakes district near Coniston Water every few years. The Altounyan children, Taqui, Susie, Titty (Mavis – a name never used by the family), Roger and Brigit were introduced to lake sailing in a pair of thirteen foot standing lugsail dinghies purchased by Ernest and Arthur, who taught, as well as very carefully watched over their sailing adventures. The dinghies were named *Swallow* and *Mavis* (changed to *Amazon*) for the books. *Swallows and Amazons* was written for the Altounyan children and their names were used except that Taqui, the eldest, became the twelve year old Captain John. So the heroes of *Swallows and Amazons* were John, Susie, Titty and Roger Walker. In later books, Bridgit became Vicky. As Dora and Barbara were both trained artists they helped Ransome with the illustrations in his books. It is interesting that Ransome chose the surname "Walker" for his central characters. He had only one daughter with Ivy, named Tabitha Walker and from whom he was later estranged. It is very likely that he harboured some regrets and a lot of guilt in that regard. Perhaps if his marriage to Ivy Walker had been successful…?

Taqui Altounyan wrote an autobiography, *Chimes from a Wooden Bell,* detailing her life between the two families, one English and the other Armenian. Ernest was raised as an English gentleman, but spent most of his life working in his father's hospital at Aleppo in Syria. Ernest's father, Aram Assadour Altounyan, was a well-respected doctor, trained at Columbia University in the USA, with an impressive reputation, and this saved him from the genocide of Armenians by the Turks In the period 1915 to 1923, a third of all Armenians in Turkey lost their lives. Ernest's mother, Harriet, was Scots Irish.

Ernest Altounyan had many literary friends in the Bloomsbury group as well as T.E Lawrence, whom he had met in 1911 and was a close friend. Lawrence read all of Ernest's poetry and sonnets. Ernest was devastated by Lawrence's death. Ernest's poetry was eventually published by Cambridge University Press.

It was in 1928, on a holiday to the Lakes country, that the Altounyan children really got to know Uncle Arthur ('Ukartha' they called him) and Aunt Genia (Evgenia). Arthur had decided to give up being a journalist and try writing children's stories. *Racundra's First Cruise* had been successfully published in 1923, By 1920, Ransome had already published twenty books including *Bohemia in London* (1907), *A History of Story Telling* (1909), *Oscar Wilde – A Critical Study* (1912) for which Ransome was sued for libel by Lord Alfred Douglas but fortunately won his case, and *Old Peter's Russian Tales* (1916). The book, *Swallows and Amazons* (1930), arrived in Aleppo in July 1930 and the family all loved it. Ransome involved the Altounyan children in suggestions for further adventures.

There seems to have been a falling out between the Ransomes and the Altounyans, perhaps due to the Ransomes pressuring to have the children educated in England rather than Syria. Maybe having no children of their own made the Ransomes put forward their suggestions. The children were being educated by correspondence from England and doing well, but the argument seemed to be mainly between Genia and Ernest, each determined to get their own way. Eventually the children were sent to England to be educated, principally because of the difficulty of meeting others of their own age in Syria. Ernest patched it up with Uncle Arthur and Aunt Genia. The Ransomes often took the children for drives in Arthur's Trojan car.

Arthur was a consummate sailor. I suspect he lived a bit in the dream world of his imagination ("off with the fairies" as they used to say before P.C. became the norm). Perhaps that's why Evgenia was such a commanding figure in his life. She could be very critical of his work, making very strong pronouncements, although book sales did not always show her to be correct. He needed her company and missed her when she wasn't around. He seems to have spent a large part of his life with recurring stomach ulcers that caused him a great deal of grief, but I suspect he was fairly contented. The books don't tell much about his life after he gave up sailing. Roger Wardell's book very nearly imparts the impression that Arthur Ransome lives on and that just perhaps, on the shores of Coniston Water he's sitting under a tree with his fishing rod or camped out on Peel Island.

Arthur Ransome was born in January 1884 and died in June 1967. Evgenia died in 1975.

In addition to *Racundra's First Cruise,* I also have in my library *The Last Englishman – The Double Life of Arthur Ransome* by Roland Chambers, and two books by Roger Wardale, who must have been a family friend: *Nancy Blackett – Under Sail with Arthur Ransome* and *Arthur Ransome on the Broads. Racundra's Third Cruise* is constructed from Ransome's incomplete notes and was never published in his lifetime.

I thought of Arthur Ransome when I climbed up through the narrow cobbled streets to the top of the hill of Old Tallinn when I briefly visited Estonia. On another occasion, I once sat in the waterside Butt and Oyster pub at Pin Mill looking out at Harry King's boatyard where Ransome had his prettiest yacht, *Selina King,* built. A 1938 photo of the visiting Australian Eleven captained by Don Bradman and autographed by all team members adorned the wall near the fireplace. I wonder if it is still there?

Lord Howe Island – Tips for Visiting

I've made five voyages to Lord Howe Island. The first, in 1981, was as crew aboard the Top Hat Topaz, sailing from Bateman's Bay and returning to Sydney. Then there were three voyages in my self-built yacht, *Aragunnu* and the last voyage in *Revolution,* our 38 foot Revolution class centreboard yacht in 1997/8. Stories of these adventures appear elsewhere.

Mounts Lidgbird and Gower looking SSW over lagoon

Lord Howe Island is every boy's dream of a perfect coral island with high mountains stretching up into the clouds, coral reefs, palm trees and yellow sandy beaches, surrounded by the bluest of water. A friend of my family's had taken a solo pre-wedding holiday there in the 1960s. In retrospect, I often wondered whether he was looking for someone else (someone better?), before making that final commitment. In those days, the journey was by flying boat out of Rose Bay and took about four hours. It was terribly romantic. His photos set my determination to go there one day.

The island is crescent-shaped, running roughly northwest to southeast with a coral reef across the crescent providing a protected lagoon anchorage with a number of moorings for visiting vessels. The anchorage is fairly shallow but deep enough for most yachts and deep enough at high tide for the regular cargo boat to get to the wharf for unloading goods. It sits on the bottom at low tide.

There are a number of passages through the fringing reef allowing entry, the North passage being nearest to the main settlement and the one most used. Several depressions in the lagoon provide deep water and moorings are laid there. Comet's Hole had the moorings for the flying boats and is located a kilometre or so out from the main beach near the small island in the centre of the lagoon. Another depression called Sylph's Hole is much closer to the shore near the North end of the lagoon and quite close to the wharf. There used to be three yacht moorings here and Topaz occupied one on my first voyage. Our rubber dinghy was punctured on coral so we had to borrow a dinghy for shore trips.

Sylph's Hole was very popular with the glass bottomed tourist boats because the coral growing on the sides was pretty and colourful. Unfortunately some selfish ignorant yachtsman lived on his yacht on one of the moorings for a few weeks and threw his rubbish over the side spoiling the area for the tourists, so the authorities removed those moorings sometime between 1981 and my next trip there in 1985.

The northwestern end of the island is unpopulated but there is a nice picnic area at North Beach and there are excellent walking tracks to the scenic spots such as The Gulch. The South-western third of the island has the two mountains. The rest of the island is part hilly, part flat, part forested and part farmland interspersed with houses, the odd shop and holiday resorts. The T intersection, not far up from the wharf, is of the road which runs around the lagoon and the road which runs across the island and this seems to be the centre of the settlement, having the community hall, the Post Office and one souvenir shop. In 1981 the telephone was here, where one could book trunk calls back to the mainland. Movies were shown in the hall once or twice a week, there being no television at that time.

The road across the island runs to Ned's Beach where lighters are stored. These were used for unloading cargo ships which anchored off the island in the early days. I don't think cargo has arrived on the island that way for quite some years although the lighters appear to be still available. Ned's Beach is popular for snorkeling and hand fish feeding.

Near Sylph's Hole was a resort called the Milky Way. Maybe it still operates but was closed for a while. In the 1980s, once or twice a week in the evenings, they had something called a fish bake. You arrived at the entrance, paid your ten dollars and took a place at a table, all in the open air. It was very crowded with what seemed to be the whole island's population present. Drinks were available from the bar. You received a plate with some chips, maybe a tiny bit of salad and a smallish piece of deep fried battered kingfish. Our newcomer friends started to grumble that the meal wasn't very good value for money. But we'd been there before and told them to be quiet and wait. Then it happened. The waiters and waitresses started appearing from the kitchen with enormous trays of deep fried battered kingfish. My mouth waters as I write this. I find it hard to describe just how delicious this stuff was. And it just kept coming and coming!! All you could eat!

Outside, it was pitch black under the tree-lined road. Some were on unlit bicycles and some had torches, but the quiet murmur of contented voices around you informed that you were not alone, staggering along weighed down by all that fish you had greedily swallowed.

Seventeen miles south-east of Lord Howe Island is Ball's Pyramid. This is a spectacular sheer spire of rock rising some 1850 feet from sea level. The interesting thing is that you can't see it from any of the settled areas of the island because the mountains block the view. We made a point of sailing around it for a closer view when leaving the island. It must be one of the most stunning natural features of the world.

For many, a voyage to Lord Howe Island is their first ocean passage away from the protection of a nearby coastline and safe anchorages. Lots of cruising folk make their first long cruise to Northern Queensland. That's fine if you have the time and it is a much harder journey than a short run across a bit of the Tasman to a real South Pacific Island.

If you are contemplating a visit, I suggest you phone the Harbour master and let them know you are planning to sail over. If you are going in a busy time such as Christmas/New Year or Easter then booking some rental bicycles might be a good idea.

You will need a chart of L.H.I. (AUS 213), and the appropriate ocean chart which covers the entire east coast of Australia to New Zealand (AUS 4620). A radio direction finder is also useful as you can home in on the aero beacon which puts out L.H. in Morse code (dit, dah, dit, dit, dit, dit, dit, dit) Take plenty of batteries for your GPS, set a waypoint just off the entrance to the North Passage, check the weather and off you go.

If you arrive at night, I suggest you wait around for daylight. No point in disturbing people at night. If the wind is strong, go around to the lee side of the island. When the sun is up, start calling "Lord Howe Maritime" on channel 16 or 12 to let them know you have arrived. The entrance through the reef at North Passage has clear leads but if you haven't been before it may be best to wait until the harbour master comes out to meet you and show you to a mooring. You may be directed by radio from the shore. Not all moorings are accessible at all states of the tide. The lagoon does experience some movement at high tide when waves break over the fringing reef. You may need your own stout ropes to tie to the mooring as the moorings don't appear to be well maintained and are made up of network of chains on the bottom. You should dive in with mask and snorkel and check what you've tied up to. The aquamarine water will be utterly clear and amaze you.

The most comfortable moorings are off Rabbit Island in the centre of the lagoon. The Comet Hole moorings are the furthest from civilisation, but are comfortable. The Dawson's Point moorings are the most accessible from shore but experience the most movement. All vessels in the lagoon are required to moor as anchoring damages the coral. There is a fee for mooring which goes towards the maintenance of the amenities block, which has a laundry, showers, toilets and water, located near the landside end of the wharf.

You can land on the main lagoon beach from the moorings at Rabbit Island and Comet's Hole, or at the launching ramp around the corner from the main wharf near Settlement Beach, from the Dawson's Point moorings. Theft is not a problem so your dinghy and outboard can be left for the day provided it is above the high tide mark and out of the way. A reliable outboard and a good sized dinghy are essential as the moorings are quite a way from the shore and it can be a wet passage if there is any breeze.

The Island is surprisingly dark at night and not all bicycles have lights, so it is wise to have a torch to see and be seen.

Mount Gower, at nearly 3000 feet high, is a full day excursion and requires a certain level of fitness. You must take the organised walk with the guide. The island is small enough to get around without a bicycle but it's better to save your energy for the places a bike can take you. There are bicycle racks near the wharf or you can leave bicycles at the bike hire shop overnight. At the time of writing there are no ATMs on the Island but there is a bank and two EFTPOS outlets. You won't find much in the way of hardware or chandlery, so you should carry all the spares you think you'll need.

The island has a good choice of restaurants, many attached to guesthouses but you should check before just turning up. The shops sell mostly touristy things but good souvenir T-shirts and the like are reasonably priced. A very good range of groceries is available and there is a well-stocked liquor store. Meat and fresh bread are available but make enquiries first. Telephones are next to the Post Office and there is a Tourist Office opposite with lots of information and brochures.

Because it is an isolated outpost of Australia with a Customs Officer, you must notify them of your arrival. It is not the same as just sailing into Broken Bay. There is no Customs Inspection if you are arriving from an Australian port.

The direct passage from Sydney to Lord Howe Island crosses two seamounts. Strong winds can dramatically alter the sea state in this vicinity and it is best to try to pass well to leeward of the seamounts. Jumping off from Port Stephens gives a more direct and shorter passage avoiding the seamounts. Winter and the months either side are the windiest but you can strike storms at any time. Storm sails are advisable. You should also practise heaving-to before you leave in case you have to wait around. It is wise to carry enough fuel to motor at least 250 miles. The worst place to lose your mast would be half way and this amount of fuel is enough to reach either end. Fuel is available on the Island but it has to be manhandled in containers.

Lord Island is a great destination.

A Little Tender behind

We have owned several inflatable dinghies over the years but my preference has always been for hard dinghies. One rough night when we ran aground on a sandbar off Corlett in Port Stephens in a stiff north-easterly with a falling tide convinced me of the value of hard dinghies. We were able to deploy our dinghy and anchor over the side in probably less than a minute. There was no furious pumping up of an inflatable and attaching a recalcitrant outboard. "Have you switched on the fuel?" A few swift strokes of the oars and the anchor was out in deep water and we eventually winched ourselves off. Sadly, this did not happen not before our line had disabled *Sunflower,* which came to our rescue (a story told elsewhere).

Inflatables have other drawbacks. The longest lasting appear to be those made by Avon. These used to be constructed from material which has Hypalon calendared on each side. Other quality brands have Hypalon on the outside and neoprene on the inside. Neoprene is more airtight than Hypalon but it may be the ability of Hypalon to leak some air that makes inflatables made from it last so long - perhaps 20+ years. These days they all seem to be made from cheaper PVC. Northern European brands such as Metzler have always been made from PVC and even Zodiac changed to PVC construction. The enemy of PVC is sunlight and in Australia we know what that means. There is however, a solution. A fitted cover made of sail cover material will allow a PVC inflatable to last for many years.

A slatted timber floor is my preference, as they are easy to roll up and one doesn't have to mess around with slabs of plywood. Some air filled floors seem rather bouncy and with no rigidity in the floor must be like walking around on a waterbed (not that I've ever tried that).

RIBs are even better but you lose the compact storage advantage which it seems to me is the whole reason for owning an inflatable in the first place. Inflatables are remarkably stable and don't mind much if you step on the pontoon when boarding. Hard dinghies are far more sensitive to weight distribution. I haven't tried rowing a RIB but I imagine they row better than other types of inflatables which are truly execrable to row with their vestigial oars. Consequently owning an inflatable without an accompanying outboard just doesn't happen. Then you have all the problems of carrying petrol. There are anchorages over a kilometre from the shore, such as in Lord Howe Island, where not having an outboard makes things very difficult, particularly at night and particularly when the wind is blowing.

Revolution to Lord Howe Island

In 1997/98, my oldest son, Douglas, suggested that a voyage to Lord Howe would be a good idea and that he'd like to take his girlfriend, Kerryn, there. Initially he wanted some other friends to go but eventually it was decided that besides Douglas and Kerryn, my other son Brian and I would go. Our life raft is a five man, so if any other Walkers came it would have to be daughter Jane or Cynthia but not both. In the event, neither came.

My first trip to the island was in 1980 or 1981, when the opportunity to crew on a Top Hat came up. Cynthia pointed out that since I was in the middle of building an ocean capable yacht, "Hadn't you better find out whether you like it not?" Such wisdom! Three other trips were made to Lord Howe Island in *Aragunnu,* my self-built yacht.

I remember the law of diminishing returns from high school economics such as when eating ice creams, each successive one becomes less enjoyable until you stop eating them. After a time, the craving returns. So it is with Lord Howe Island.

We didn't need a lot of preparation as I had made everything on *Revolution* as reliable as I could. I was interested to know what sort of ocean crossing performance I could expect from a centreboard yacht. With some extra batteries and a Rutland wind generator installed, we had 500 ampere hours of battery capacity on what is a fairly greedy electrical system, even though we have no fridge. A few extra safety items were added, such as new flares and we were ready.

We left on the tail of a southerly on Boxing Day and made rapid progress under well-reefed sails. The wind was strong with gusts up to 30 knots, and the seas were lively with some waves breaking aboard that revealed lots of deck leaks. I'd overfilled the fuel tank and the combination of leaking diesel and shallow bilges had the sole awash making it very slippery in the main cabin. For only the second time in my sailing career, I was sick. Mind you, relief can be instantaneous once you've emptied your stomach but I must say I've never met anyone who enjoys vomiting.

In the small hours one night, I came to the realisation that we had no steering. *Revolution's* steering works by means of a hydraulic ram mounted on the transom and connected to the rudder. The four bolts holding the ram onto the transom had sheared. Luckily, I had a good selection of bolts on board and we were underway again after forty five anxious minutes which included Doug hanging over the stern with a spanner doing up nuts while Brian held his legs and I attended to the other end of the bolts inside the stern cabin.

The wind swung around to the South East and our path on the chart resembled a big curve taking us to the north of the Island. To get there we had to face working to windward. We sailed and motor-sailed, arriving on the fourth day. One of the frustrating things about Lord Howe is, because it is so tall, you can see it from a long way off and it can seem to take forever to get there.

Before leaving home, I'd rung Clive Wilson on the Island and was advised to call Lord Howe Maritime on VHF Channel 12 or 16 when I arrived. Clive was his usual welcoming self and directed us to a mooring off Rabbit Island. Clive told me he was now semi-retired and his son Campbell had taken over the bike hire business. For a man who is 65 this year, Clive has astonishing energy. He'd be up early and out fishing, driving tourists around during the day, last boat back with buckets of fish in the evening as the sun set. Somewhere in there were some games of lawn bowls as well. It's definitely a healthy lifestyle.

Lord Howe is a wonderful place and little changes there. We visited Ned's Beach and swam with and fed the fish, we visited the Valley of the Shadows and Middle Beach, North Beach and The Gulch and walked amongst the banyan trees, kentia and pandanus palms. Doug, Kerryn and Brian did the climbing tour of Mount Gower - I am not fit enough for that. We cycled about. The Lagoon Store has become Trader Nicks Cafe but, sadly, Capella South no longer serves lunch to non-guests.

The weather conditions were perfect for our entire stay. I observed one interesting phenomenon. The Island is in drought at present and there is a water shortage. Yet, out on the mooring and at least a kilometre from shore, we experienced two heavy rain showers which did not reach the main Island.

They say all good things must end, although I'm not sure why, and we headed for home on Sunday 4th January. The weather station predicted a southerly change in a couple of days so I planned to take advantage of the prevailing easterly and head south past the seamounts before turning east hopefully picking the southerly to enable us to sail on a broad reach to Sydney. The best laid plans can go awry. The southerly hit hard before we had gone far enough south. We struggled on for a few hours but *Revolution's* windward ability in strong winds and choppy water is not good, so I had to give it up and make a run between the seamounts. I observed three very distinct changes in the sea state with no obvious change in the wind. This was when we crossed over onto the shelf, which is to the north of the Taupo Seamount. The second was when we left the shelf and went back over deep water. The third was when we crossed onto the continental shelf as we neared the NSW coastline. The sea state above the shelves was extremely rough with heaped up breaking waves everywhere. I had been able to accurately plot our position on the chart with the GPS and knew exactly where we were in relation to the seabed contours. Clearly, areas where the sea bottom changes dramatically in depth are places to be avoided in poor conditions as they are where a small vessel could easily be overwhelmed.

The lagoon from Mt Gower

The crew: Kerryn, Doug and Brian

We did a lot of motoring on the way home as the wind speed dropped. The only worrying moment came in the middle of the night (why do bad things always happen in the middle of the night?), when Brian called me up to advise that the engine exhaust was emitting a lot of blue smoke. I pondered on this for a while and decided that we had been running it for too long without sufficient load. Diesels don't like this. I pushed up the engine revs and by morning the smoke had stopped. We'd monitored the oil pressure to ensure we hadn't run low on oil.

The Rutland wind generator was a great success on the Island in the steady wind conditions but was of not much use on the downwind stages of the voyage.

Finally, drawing some conclusions about *Revolution* as an ocean going vessel, I would say that structurally and rig wise it is very sound. Due to the high centre of gravity, it has a slow roll and is very comfortable. The galley and chart table areas are easy to work at and the accommodation and space in general, is very good. The long waterline produces fast speeds. The cockpit is a problem in that it scoops up water from along the side deck and fills far too readily, overwhelming the small drains. The washboards need to be kept in most of the time. The latches I fitted hold them in place. Windward ability in choppy seas is a bit of a concern, despite having the weight to plow through. I guess that this may be a problem for all centreboard yachts. The leaks can be fixed. The big mainsail requires a lot of strength to reef.

All in all, the voyage to Lord Howe Island was a great success.

The Aborted Voyage

Greg Shaw put in quite a lot of time, money and effort for his voyage aboard *Shawfire*, his wing-keeled Wayworld 45. We had been planning the trip for some months. All the cushions were refilled so that they were more comfortable. Years of use tends to flatten foam filled items. Greg had stern and side boarding ladders made and fitted. As Greg lives aboard, carloads of stuff had to be taken ashore. A number of jobs were done by shipwrights and electricians, including refrigeration repairs, making and installing a new hot water tank, fitting a 1500 watt inverter and wiring for 240 volts AC. New batteries were installed. Sails were repaired and a minor repair made to the boom. Greg bought a new rubber ducky and a 15 hp outboard and a Coden HF radio.

Shawfire is craned out of the backyard, Gladesville

Greg purchased a Garmin 48 GPS. computerised, hydraulic ram actuated, self-steering was fitted. Lenore looked after provisioning of food lockers, frig and freezer. I supplied charts, a second spare GPS, a Walker Trailing Log, a wind generator and a freshly serviced five-man life raft. I also fitted jackstays along the side decks. My rubber ducky and 2 hp outboard were stowed below.

After fuelling, watering and the last minute storing and packing of a mountain of gear, we left Westport Marina at 0900 on Saturday 15th, 2003. Aboard were Greg and his son Matthew, Lenore Grunsell (a mutual friend), Cynthia and myself. We passed through the heads around 1100 and streamed the log. The wind allowed us to set a waypoint to the north of the seamounts. The behaviour of the ocean in the vicinity of the seamounts is like that in very shoaling waters.

Predictably the wind became stronger as time wore on so we reefed both main and jib. There was a lot of spray but *Shawfire* handled it all well.

Sometime on Sunday afternoon, Lenore noticed a lot of water coming out of the bottom locker in the forward cabin. We investigated and found water streaming out of an opening in a large pipe running through the locker. The lockers on either side were dry. A visit to the foredeck confirmed that the anchor locker and the sail locker which the anchor locker drains into were both full of water to deck level. The drains at the bottom of the sail locker, under four feet of water, were either blocked or unable to cope with the ingress of water. The weight of water in the bow caused it to bury itself in every wave. The bilge pumps were keeping up with the flow of water into the main cabin and the water wasn't getting deeper. At this point, Greg made the decision to turn back. He started the engine and we pointed for home. The log showed we had covered ninety miles.

An unusual design feature of *Shawfire* is that the fresh water tank breathers exit in the anchor locker. With the locker flooded, the fresh water tanks were sucking in saltwater each time the fresh water taps were turned on. The pipe starting in the anchor locker and running through the boat almost as far as the chart table is a conduit for electric cables. It was thought to be sealed but clearly wasn't. Water was being conducted into the boat at a rate similar to that of a tap being turned on. With no limber holes in the lockers, not all the water could drain into the bilge. Later, when Matthew and I bucketed out all the water with a 15 litre plastic bucket, I estimated we had moved over a tonne of water.

We could have kept going as we weren't in any danger of foundering. We could have cleared the sail locker and found what was happening to the drains and tried to block the water entry to the conduit, but having covered less than a quarter of the journey and the coast still relatively close, it seemed the sensible thing to turn back. Besides we only had a spare twenty-litre drum of fresh water. Then there were the imponderables such as having a spell of bad weather and whether our efforts to reduce the ingress could have failed. Continuing placed too much reliance on the engine and the electrics. A failure of either could have tipped the balance of probabilities towards sinking.

It is marvellous to sail on a vessel on which everything, bar sail reefing, winching and furling, works to the touch of a button. However electricity requirements are enormous with electric toilets, autopilot, radios, fresh and saltwater pumps, fans lights, TV, video, microwave oven, inverter and two CPAP machines (Cynthia and Greg both use them) especially if something goes wrong. The house battery capacity of 440 ampere hours seems fine and ample, but an emergency can cut into this quickly as happened to us. If, for one reason or another, the engine is lost, then the functioning of the whole boat is threatened.

It took twenty-five hours to get back to the coast and, not surprisingly, the wind was on the nose most of the way. We spent a few days in Broken Bay eating up some of the larder and generally relaxed. I don't know whether Greg has been turned off ocean sailing.

Launching the Wayworld 45, *Shawfire* at River Quays, Parramatta River

A Skippered Yacht Charter in the Ionian Islands 2015

Sterling Hayden, US actor and author, wrote that as we age "the dreams of youth lie gathering dust on the shelves of patience". When Cynthia and I set sail on our South Pacific journey in 1986, I always envisaged further yacht voyages to distant lands. Of course, life got in the way and various barriers delayed and then prevented me/us following the dreams. One can crash through the barriers as they are mostly illusionary mental ones, but the price to pay is that compromises and sacrifices must be made. Lucky is the sailor whose partner shares those dreams. Most have their own dreams. As the years pass, the need to ensure financial security in one's old age becomes paramount and the ties to family can be the hardest to set aside. Then age itself starts to impose and health issues arise.

With the realisation that the time left is diminishing, one starts to prioritise the dreams. Americans conveniently call it a "bucket list". Items requiring a level of physicality no longer available are struck off. Cynthia and I have always shared a love of travel which had us on a Greek Island yacht charter with the Mills and Emerys in 1992, canal boat charters in France in 1997, Holland in 2007, Italy (Venice) 2010, two cruise ship voyages to the Med in 2013 and the South Pacific in 2015, and on long motorcycle rides over much of Australia and in the Western US States in 2009. But I still hanker to sail a yacht to islands unknown to us. As I near the end of my seventh decade I am sure I am still able to meet any physical demands sailing may throw at me, but I'm not so sure about Cynthia.

A small ad in *Sydney Afloat* caught my eye and the idea of a skippered yacht charter in the Ionian Islands of Western Greece took form. With surprising alacrity, our friends Serge and Charmain Boyakovsky, offered to accompany us. On Friday the 18th September we caught a ferry from Corfu to Gaia Harbour on Paxos to meet Tony and Mady (Madeleine) Sharp, the NZ owners of *Ripple Effect*, a Beneteau Cyclades 43 sloop.

For the next two weeks, we explored little harbours and anchorages on Levkas, Paxos, Cephalonia, Megonisi and Ithaka. Tony and Mady have been doing this for a few years, taking guests to Croatia and Greece. They have refined and developed their service making them the perfect hosts.

The *Beneteau* is ideal, having two rear double cabins with ensuites and ample storage. Twin steering wheels make movement to the stern and across the narrow gangplank (Tony refuses to call it a 'passerolle') easy, even for slightly unstable senior citizens like us. Tony made Mediterranean mooring look simple and guided us to some very scenic places with excellent tavernas. Sailing with someone who knows the area guarantees you will see the best spots. Tony and Mady have catered for a wide variety of yachting pursuits chosen by their various charterers, so I trusted that their knowledge would enable us to pack much more into two weeks, than a bareboat charter could possibly have provided us with.

Ripple Effect

Unfortunately, dear readers, ours was their final Ionian charter. They checked out of Greece for Sicily and will recommence chartering in that area in 2016. I am sure it won't be long before they have sussed out some delightful places to visit around Sicily or Malta. Look for their advertisement in *Sydney Afloat*. (Note: In 2021, they are now retired and are living in Auckland, NZ)

Our first night was spent in Gaia Harbour on Paxos. This is a narrow channel between Paxos and a smaller island, which shallows at the southern end sufficiently to close it off that way. The next day, with no wind, we motored down to Levkas and through the channel to Levkas Marina. There are many charter fleets stationed here. The swing bridge at the start of the channel opens on the hour and our timing was perfect. Apparently the offer of a permanent bridge was refused as Levkas would no longer be an isolated island and certain tax and other advantages would be lost. We explored Levkas town after dinner and next morning pushed on to Vathi Harbour on Meganisi after a swim stop at Skorpina. We passed Onassis's island now leased to AK47 toting Russians – do not attempt to go near where they moor.

"Vathi" apparently means harbour so they are many "Vathis" throughout Greece. Moored four yachts along from us was the man himself, the doyen of Mediterranean yacht cruising, Rod Heikel, author of the best Mediterranean Pilots. As fellow New Zealanders, Tony spent some time aboard Rod's Alan Warwick designed yacht and had his new Sicilian Pilot autographed.

Gaia Harbour, Paxos

The weather had become cloudy and there were some showers about so we stayed another night, leaving the following day for Sivota Harbour on Levkas, where Tony had booked a space on the Stavros Taverna pontoon. We enjoyed an excellent meal looking out over the little harbour as the sun set and lights were switched on. Cynthia and I were drinking our favourite Greek tipple Ouzo "12" but house white and red wines were always very drinkable, as was the local beer.

We sailed to Agia Eufimia on Cefalonia and stayed three nights as the weather closed in and we had some very heavy showers. Cynthia and I caught a taxi to Sami, the capital of Cefalonia and setting for the movie "Captain Corelli's Mandolin". We each ate an ice cream.

On Saturday 26th we left early for Vathi Harbour on Ithaka, supposedly the home of Homer's fabled hero, Ulysses. Rod Heikel's pilot mentions recent research which suggests that a large peninsula on the western side of Cephalonia was a separate island 3000 years ago and matches more closely Homer's description of Ithaka, than the present island. Perhaps archaeological research and some digging will turn up some real evidence. Ithaka did not seem as prosperous as the other islands which, because of tourism, are not feeling the depth of the Greek financial crisis as severely as on the mainland. We moved on to Kioni in the north of Ithaka, which was a very pretty little harbour – like all the other places we visited. We lunched and dined at the tavernas.

The next day, Tony took *Ripple Effect* in close to the cave on Meganisi, but we elected not to swim in, and later tied up to a hotel pontoon in Nidri Harbour on Levkas. We made use of the hotel swimming pool and washing machines. The lass in the nearby chandlery was from Melbourne, with a Greek father and Australian mother.

Departure was at 6:30 the next morning for the longish passage up through Levkas channel (first cut by the Romans) and bridge, and on to Monganisi on Paxos. I was happy to helm for a few hours although the breeze weakened during the morning. This was another beautiful bay dominated by a taverna. We ate at a table under the trees by the beach and watched the shadows lengthen into the night. It was another memorable evening. We didn't partake of the dancing and partying that continued well into the night with the distant notes of Zorba drifting across the water. That was for the young and younger at heart.

A 7:30 am start was needed for the six hour passage back to Corfu, where we tied up at Gouvia Marina for two nights. This is another big marina. Things were starting to wind down with only another two or three weeks left in the tourist season. We taxied to Empress Elizabeth's Achillion Palace, explored Old Corfu town, ate a terrific dinner at the Marina Café and said our farewells to Tony, Mady and *Ripple Effect* on Friday morning, returning to our hotel near the airport. It had been a superb two weeks.

I suppose the question to answer is "Was it all worth it?" In short, yes. Costwise it was comparable to and no more expensive than a big ship cruise from Holland America, Royal Caribbean, etc. and probably a lot less expensive if you take any of the guided tours offered by the big ships. "Would I do it again?" Again, "Yes," but with reservations. I think we were very lucky that Tony and Mady were such brilliant hosts and that *Ripple Effect* was perfect for six people. Finally, "What would I complain about?" As always, time flashes by; the end comes quickly and one tries to preserve memories aided by the photographic record. I wouldn't have changed anything. Serge and Charmain were excellent travelling companions, but we knew that when we set out. Perhaps I should have jumped in the water more; the water was very clean and clear everywhere we went and I guess I would have liked to have travelled lighter, but packing mistakes are almost inevitable, aren't they?

At the end of two weeks you feel as if you'd just had a sample taste and there should be a lot more. Many Europeans, particularly the British, keep their yachts in big marinas on Corfu, Levkas and elsewhere, spending from around April through to late October amongst the islands. Winter brings rain and stronger winds but temperatures are always above freezing in Corfu, so one could sail all year although it seems few do. Many British expats live permanently on Corfu. There seems to be an abundance of fairly late model ex-charter yachts for sale in the islands. Yachts such as the Bavaria 40, 41 and 42 can be bought for well under A$100,000. Smaller yachts are for sale for much less. I saw a Beneteau Cyclades 43 for fifty thousand Euros (less than A$90,000). I would imagine keeping a yacht there for a few years could be a viable proposition, and this is just such a fabulous part of the world to explore.

USES FOR A CAT ON A YACHT
— AS A FENDER —

FIRST IN A SERIES: THIS ENTRY FROM SHELAGH AND EMILE
(TELL ME THE USAGE AND I'LL ILLUSTRATE IT. ED.)

Our Friends, Greg and Ann Coonan

Greg and I met at University in 1975, where we were both attending as mature-age students (note the distinction between 'mature' and 'mature-age'). We were both teachers and were upgrading our qualifications to get into school counselling, which we managed in 1976.

(From L to R) Greg Coonan, Bruce Walker, Ann Coonan and Cynthia Walker

Cynthia and I had a small keelboat, a Southerly 23. On one memorable occasion, I invited Greg and Ann to sail with us from Broken Bay down to Sydney Harbour. You've probably heard how some folk turn green while suffering from mal-de-mer. Well, Greg actually did turn that colour. He held his eyes fixed on the horizon, "Don't make me look down. Don't make me look in the cabin." My thoughts at the time were: 'Here was clearly someone entirely unsuited to life on the ocean wave'. How wrong could I be?

We received appointments on the New South Wales South Coast. Greg was placed at Ulladulla and me at Bega. I had already made up my mind to build a yacht and started in early 1979. Greg had grown up at Bondi, and been involved in surfing and the like, all his life. Ann came from Avalon. I didn't think they'd take to sailing yet Greg built a Mosquito Catamaran and taught the family to sail. Earlier he had also owned several catamarans, including a Hobie 16, which we memorably sailed on Jervis Bay in 20 knot winds for about four kilometers on a single hull, with Paul aged about 8, my son Douglas aged 3, and me, clinging to the flying hull with teeth clenched and eyeballs popping out. Greg was helming.

In 1983, Greg and I both took up appointments in Sydney. We agreed to meet at Easter at the Basin where Greg would be camped with his catamaran and the Walkers would be aboard the newly launched *Aragunnu*. The Coonans came aboard and poked around looking in lockers and testing out bunks. They were sold and within weeks they bought *Harmony*, a Spacesailer 24. The world of yacht cruising would never be the same again.

Aragunnu rafted with *Harmony*, Fame Cove

Throughout 1983, the Coonans taught themselves all about sailing yachts. At Christmas, they decided to cruise to Port Stephens and we accompanied them. It was another of those passages which stick in one's memory, taking more than 24 hours (largely due to the slowness of *Aragunnu*) and all sorts of adventures before finally reaching Nelson Bay. By radio contact, Ann told us that the Coonans did a lot of vomiting on that passage. Not a good indicator of future accomplishments, one would think in retrospect. After exploring Port Stephens they headed up the Myall River to the Lakes. Another unforgettable incident was when Leigha, just two years old, fell off the back of *Harmony*, was rescued by her brother Paul, and both were picked up by a passing power boat. By now, Greg and Ann were meeting many other cruising folk. (Greg is short for 'gregarious') Some breakages on the trip back to Broken Bay soon had Greg thinking about a bigger boat. During 1984, Greg rang to say he'd met a fellow who had suggested he join his yacht club. The chap's name was Col Haste and the club was the Coastal Cruising Club. So I accompanied Greg to a meeting where we were both struck with the friendliness and camaraderie, thus beginning an association which continues to this day.

Greg and Ann upgraded from *Harmony*, buying an almost pristine Adams 31 (centre cockpit) which they named *Nanook* (spelt backwards it is 'Koonan'). *Nanook* was the Inuit Eskimo in Robert Flaherty's ground-breaking 1922 documentary *Nanook of the North*. I was never sure that Greg actually knew that when he christened the Adams. The name *Nanook* was providential in view of their later voyage in *Matatua* to Alaska, the land of the Eskimos. Greg informed me that it was his Dad's stage name from when he appeared in the Australian movie, *Forty Thousand Horsemen*.

By 1985, Greg had decided that he was ready for an ocean voyage. For Sydney-siders, the obvious choice for those with limited time is Lord Howe Island. Greg chose the August September school holidays and, with a crew comprising Greg, his son Paul, Dick Warburton (a fellow School Counsellor), and Ron Doughton, the Deputy Principal of Ulladulla Public School, they set off from Pittwater. The journey started well but the winds blew up to over fifty knots and huge seas of twenty or more feet tested their resolve.

The Walkers accompanied them in our yacht. It was *Aragunnu's* first trip to the island.

We spent a few days exploring the island before a savage storm that lasted three days blew in from the south-west. At the height of the storm in the middle of the night, Greg's mooring broke. Masses of shallow coral lay directly downwind. Fortunately, earlier in the day, Greg had donned facemask and surveyed the dubious ground tackle of the mooring and, being cautious, had dropped his own anchor. This anchor finally grabbed in their perilous flight backwards, stopping them mere metres from nasty coral outcrops.

Being a loyal employee of the Education Department (as were both the other adult crew-members), Greg elected to risk the North Passage on the Wednesday evening with just four days to get back to Sydney. The wind had dropped but the seas were still big. The North Passage seemed, from the headland, to be relatively smooth. *Nanook* headed out. A wave set reached the passage at the same time as *Nanook* and ten foot high breaking rollers swept in. *Nanook* almost stood on its propeller as Greg gunned the engine to get through. This may well have been the most dramatic moment in all their sailing adventures over the years to that time. The sea was extremely rough until they got off the geological shelf on which Lord Howe lies. The trip from then on to home was an anticlimax with lots of motoring in gentle breezes, flat seas and comfortably warm sunshine.

Greg and Ann were now well into the swing of the Coastal Cruising Club, attending most sailaways and meetings. Although a keen sportsman, footballer and then P.E. teacher, Greg is a gentle fellow and found some aspects of school counselling trying and stressful, so in 1986 he decided to take some leave at the end of first term and try some real cruising: destination Tonga.

There seemed to be a reluctance to set off as they found more excuses to do last minute jobs, but finally they were away. Another of those great dramatic moments in Greg's life occurred when eschewing the inconvenience of his harness, when *Nanook* lurched to an unexpected wave and impetuous Greg fell overboard. He managed to grab a lifeline as he went over and held on for dear life until Ann, Paul and Joanne could help him back aboard. It was 12th May, his birthday. One suspects that from then on, Greg put up with the restrictions of his harness without complaint. They cleared customs from Lord Howe Island – an idea Greg had which he believed would be more convenient than clearing from Watson's Bay.

GREG COONAN OVERBOARD MID-TASMAN

They then sailed to Raoul Island – the only inhabited island in the Kermadecs to the north of New Zealand. They met the men at the weather station there and sailed on to Tongatapu and the capital Nukualofa. From there, they cruised north through the Hai Pai group of low coral islands to Vava'U, the most northerly group of Tongan islands. They had many adventures on the way, meeting other cruising folk and collecting their first infected coral cuts.

They cruised for some three weeks around the various beauty spots of the islands around Vava'U. Aboard *Aragunnu*, the Walkers joined them for the next four weeks and they then set out together for Fiji, sailing through the Lau Group to Suva. After a few days, which included sightseeing trips into the central mountains, they sailed west around the south coast of Viti Levu to Bengga, once a big volcano, the crater of which is breached to form a huge harbour. The cruise continued to the drier west coast side of Viti Levu where they stayed at Lautoka, visiting Nadi by bus. They then pushed on to the holiday resort of Dick's Place where *Nanook's* name was carved into the ceiling of the bar. The Coonans became members of the Musket Cove Yacht Club. They continued north to explore the Yasawas and were entertained in various villages, explored underwater caves and drank a lot of anaesthetising kava.

One memorable adventure involved a sixteen year old native lass, who cadged a lift on *Nanook* to a neighbouring island but once aboard thought she would stay for the trip back to Australia. Greg had a few sleepless nights thinking the locals might assume she had been kidnapped and her kinfolk would soon be setting out in war canoes to come to her rescue. Skilled diplomacy won the day and, with the Chief's help, Greg landed her in one of the villages. Perhaps the people of the islands had tired of her and didn't want this troublesome, mischievous, young, although muscular and strapping, female either. The Coonans never found out either way. It's hard to imagine but that young woman is well into adulthood by now and probably has grandchildren.

Customs were cleared in Lautoka, and *Nanook* sailed into the Bay of Islands, New Zealand, nine days later. It was fairly uneventful although they saw a big shark following them about halfway through the voyage. Opua was the first point of contact where NZ Customs thoroughly inspected *Nanook*.

The Bay of Islands is a pretty place and there is plenty to do there with interesting towns scattered around. The tail of a hurricane lashed the northern end of NZ and the Coonans had a few anxious moments with re-anchoring at the height of the storm but all was well in the end. *Nanook* headed south, exploring Kawai Island and other delightful little harbours and anchorages along the way. The huge Westhaven Marina in Auckland Harbour provided a safe berth for the yachts and the Coonans and Walkers flew to Christchurch to pick up a six berth motorhome (there were ten of us so it was slightly crowded!) One wit in the CCC who visited NZ during this time, christened the motorhome "Nonookie") for an exploration of the South Island. Later, the Coonans sailed back to the Bay of Islands and eventually cleared customs in Whangerei (a story in itself) for Australia, which they reached in early January. They had sailed well over 5000 ocean miles. It was time to upgrade to a larger yacht, so *Nanook* was put on the market.

Former CCC Member, Keith Inns had built an *Adams* 40 out of cold moulded epoxy-glued oregon in his backyard at Concord. They'd sailed in a number of Club Sailaways but had decided that yacht cruising was not for them. He had some trouble selling the yacht because it wasn't as fancy as the buyers who looked at it wanted. Fortuitously, Greg Coonan, wanting a larger yacht and being a fan of Joe Adams' designs (Joe had an office in Newport at the time and had involvement in the building of *Matatua*), came along and made Keith an offer which he accepted. Greg and Ann became the owners of *Matatua*.

Greg served another year on the Committee of the CCC as Pittwater Cruising Officer, then the next era of Coonan sailing adventures began. *Matatua* is a beautifully built, solid and comfortable vessel with laminated frames and timbers throughout. Greg, always on the lookout for a bargain, realised how lucky he was to get it. Over the next few years, Greg and Ann attended many sailaways up and down the coast. Like most yacht owners, Greg was always improving his vessel. They were not prolific contributors to The Mainsheet but they wrote a very nice piece called 'Cruising on Lake Macquarie' about their participation in the CCC 1988 Christmas Sailaway.

Late in 1990, Greg had had enough of the NSW Department of Education and applied for a school counsellor position in Queensland, where they are called Guidance Officers, receiving higher pay and higher status than in NSW. He was appointed to Kirwan High School in Townsville. The CCCA farewelled Greg and Ann in the February 1991 issue of Coastal Cruising Club journal, The Mainsheet.

I wrote the following:

"Greg and Ann are well known club personalities. That has a great deal to do with Greg's humour and their friendly personalities. It also has much to do with his extreme thriftiness in all things yachting. The humour is that yachting and money saving are mutually exclusive, but Greg hasn't realised it yet. Greg is a person of contrasts – where would you find someone so keen on a bargain and half of a couple of the most generous people you could ever meet? You'd be hard put to find better cruising companions."

As true today as it was then. Mind you, as the children of Great Depression era parents, like Greg and me, we were imbued with the need to be careful with money and find the security of Government jobs.

Greg took *Matatua* to Townsville with a crew comprising Dick Warburton, Ann's brother Alan Cosgrave, and another friend, Ron Doughton, Deputy Principal of Ulladulla Public School.

Greg and Ann lived aboard *Matatua* in the Breakwater Marina, Townsville, during 1991, 1992 and 1993. They made various cruises to islands south and north of Townsville, including a memorable one, with the five Walkers aboard, to Dunk Island via the Palm Islands (Orpheus and Fantome), Hinchinbrook (Zoe Bay), and Gould Islands returning via the inside passage of Hinchinbrook, and Magnetic Island, where they met with friends and fellow C.C.C. Members, Brian and Jill Robinson, who wintered each year on the Island.

Greg and Ann saved hard and started to plan a voyage to Alaska. They left Townsville on the 17th December 1993. This is right in the middle of the Cyclone Season so they needed to cross the Tropics quickly.

The weather Bureau gave them a window and seven and a half days later they arrived in Gizo, Solomon Islands. It was Christmas Day and the heat made them think of Townsville as a winter resort. Their three children, Paul, Joanne and Leigha were aboard. They explored Morovo Lagoon and New Georgia and then headed east to Kiribati. From there they sailed north to the Marshall Islands.

From the Marshalls, they made a 34 day passage to Sitka, Alaska, arriving in May. Again, Greg spent a birthday at sea. Nature provided the entertainment with spectacular scenery, glaciers, hot springs and wildlife with seals, sea lions, black bears, bears fishing for salmon, and whales. The radar Greg had installed before leaving should have been invaluable in the frequently foggy conditions, however, *Matatua* encountered no fog.

Greg marvelled about the bargain the Americans made buying Alaska from the Russians for seven million dollars. Leigha caught a 40lb king salmon which they shared with other cruisers.

Matatua wintered in Sidney, Vancouver Island, and the family bought a car and caravan to tour Canada, the USA and Mexico. By late 1994, they were in Miami, Florida.

The family explored Skagway, Whitehorse, Dawson and the Klondike before moving south. An encounter with a fuel tanker truck destroyed their caravan. They sailed the inside passage from Ketchican, exploring the Queen Charlotte Islands and others on their way south. Fierce currents caused a few problems and Greg found himself in the water a couple of times. So cold was the water, Greg called it 'spanner water' and claimed his voice had risen to soprano. (If you don't know what spanner water is, you may need to ask someone, but it means 'very, very cold'.)

In the northern spring of 1995, Australia and home beckoned. They passed through Juan de Fuca Straits on their way to the Marquesas Islands 3500 nautical miles away. Yet again Greg spent a birthday at sea. (I am sure he does this so he doesn't have to pay for a party.) The voyage took 29 days. They explored Nuku Hiva and Ua Pau and then they sailed on to Ahe and Rangiroa in the Tuamotus. The expense of French Polynesia and the tourism caused them to by-pass Papeete and sail direct to Moorea and Cook's Bay. Huahini, Raiatea and Tahaa and their very deep anchorages were next, followed by Bora Bora, which they loved despite the tourism. Greg complained about how expensive it all was and how he wouldn't be rushing back there. A six day sail took them to isolated Suvarov Island, which is part of the Cook Islands. They sailed into Brisbane on the 7th November having enjoyed Fiji and especially Kandavu.

Greg and Ann were awarded the Coastal Cruising Club's Blue Water Award at the 1995 Commodore's Dinner.

Greg returned to work in Brisbane, as did Ann. *Matatua*, now moored in the Brisbane River at Bulimba, has made more voyages north exploring the islands and coast of Queensland, as well as many trips to the Gold Coast.

Greg took a redundancy package when his age made him eligible and started building a Farrier 31 Trimaran. His love of speed from those catamarans he owned and sailed years ago has resurfaced. Greg's workmanship is, as expected, superb. Mind you, good craftsmen can always find faults (invisible to others) in their own work and Greg was always modest about his own abilities. *Matatua* received a new engine and continues to perform beautifully. It took Greg ten years to finish his trimaran. Ian Farrier visited and commented on Greg's superb workmanship. Greg convinced Ann to stay working until he had finished the tri, claiming it wouldn't take long to build – perhaps six months. Greg and Ann cruised the trimaran for a few years but eventually sold it and bought a Top Hat. Although they still own *Matatua*, they now have a trailer-sailer.

Anatomy of a Cruising Yacht
So you want to go cruising?

You want some help with selecting a yacht and what you'll need Just about everyone has an opinion on the perfect cruising yacht. I'm no different from anyone else but I have studied everything to do with boats that I could lay my hands on for the last thirty years and sailed over ten thousand miles on a variety of boats off the coast and on the ocean. I am humbled by people who have sailed prodigious distances in yachts. I actually like sailing on the ocean. I don't yearn for the voyage to be over and I do get a great sense of personal achievement after a cruise where personal resources and skills have prevailed. A crowning moment of my life was the day (August 8th, 1986) I sailed into Port Maurelle, Vava'U, Tonga, with my wife and three small children, after twenty six days at sea non-stop from Sydney, Australia. We were aboard my 27 foot yacht, which I had designed and built in the splendid isolation of country New South Wales. I felt I had done something as a designer, a boat builder, a navigator with sextant, almanac, tables and compass, and as a sailor. Everything self-taught.

There are some basic questions which you have to ask yourself:
1. How long do you want to cruise for?
2. Where do you want to cruise?
3. How many people aboard?

You can divide this up into <u>very short term</u>, viz. weekends and holidays up to a couple of weeks; <u>short term</u>, viz up to say six months; <u>medium term</u>, say six months to three years; and <u>long term</u> or indefinitely.

Back to your future boat:
If we're talking <u>very short term</u> then I'd say buy whatever you like that you can afford. Remember that it is nice to be able to stand up in the cabin. But there is no size limit. Some people cruise in a sailing dinghy of around sixteen feet, with a flat floor and a boom tent. How much sailing have you done? It is nice to be able to have a boat that sails sweetly (I'll address this later when I discuss hull design). Most trailer-sailers come into this category.

On the other hand, if we are talking <u>short term,</u> then you probably need a boat of around 25 feet or more. If you plan on being aboard for six months then it means you'll being doing some significant coastal hops. So the boat will need to be strong. In Australia, boats like Top Hats and Compass 28/29s are a good choice of proven small designs which have sailed considerable distances. (Jan and Ian Mitchell sailed around the world in a mark I Top Hat.) There are lesser known others like the Duncanson 29 and any of the 1970s IOR half tonners are also good and plentiful to choose from. (Endeavour 27/28/30, Pion, Adams 31, Viking, Spacesailer 27, Easterly 30, Nantucket 30, S&S 30, MW 32, Cole 31, Carter 30, Santana 28, Peterson 30, and lots of others.)

Aragunnu sailing in Pittwater

Putting a bottom limit on it, I wouldn't consider a boat of less than around 5000 to 6000 lbs displacement (two and half tons plus). It can be done in boats like the S80 or M27 but they are fairly lightly constructed. For short term cruising I would test a boat's hull strength like this: Find a large flattish part of the hull eg (sides near the bow) and see if you can get it to flex by pushing it in and out with your hand, pumping it. If it does flex, consider that if you take a piece of material and bend it back and forth it will eventually fracture. Some materials will withstand the flexing a lot more than others (e.g. timber outlasts aluminium in this type of contest), but it will break. Older glass boats often have hairline fractures along lines of flex. Look for them. Folkboats are possible (Anne Gash circumnavigated in a wooden one), but they are tight for space. In this category you can also go as big as you can afford. Similarly, interior layouts are not especially critical, as most nights are spent in anchorages, marinas and the like, and only the very occasional night is spent at sea.

In the area of medium term, we are starting to think about major voyages which may involve an ocean crossing. You will need a boat that is capable of withstanding whatever the weather is capable of throwing at you in the area you are intending to sail. You can do a world circumnavigation in less than two years. The reality is that bigger boats do not get tossed around as much as little boats in the ocean by virtue of their size and greater weight. In general, they are steadier and faster. So it really comes down to what you can afford.

Before proceeding, I will set out some general parameters for your consideration.

    a. I wouldn't set out across an ocean without at least 70 gallons of water in at least two or more separate tanks (no showers for the crew on this boat!). If, for some reason, one of your tanks fractures, then you can get by on 30 gallons but I wouldn't want to try it on fifteen gallons (67 litres). You can survive for months without food but only for a few days without water. Yes, you can take a water maker, but ask yourself what you would do if it breaks down.

    b. You need proper sea berths. These will be as wide as the widest crew member plus a couple of inches, a couple of inches longer than the tallest crew member and parallel to the centreline of the boat. There should be some means of keeping the sleeper in the bunk (a lee cloth) for whichever way the boat is heeling. Preferably the bunks should be located aft of the mast as bunks forward of the mast tend to experience too much up and down motion. Bunks nearest the centre of the waterline will experience least motion. It would be nice to have at least one sea berth for each crew member but you will need at least as many as there are crew less one for the person on watch (four crew need at least three sea berths).

    c. If the boat you've been looking at doesn't have the above two minimum features, look elsewhere!

There are also some general rules of the sea which you should know and apply:

(i)   Outside of an acid bath, or the interior of a non-extinct volcano, the ocean is one of the most corrosive environments in nature.

(ii)   The ocean is constantly in motion and thus everything is moving and subject to wear even if it is not being used. The ocean wears away rocks.

(iii)   Because of the above two points, everything mechanical, which has moving parts and metal (e.g. engines, self-steering gear, rudders and steering, sheaves and blocks, wire rigging and rigging screws, sail furlers, sheet winches, hydraulics, manual anchor winches, stoves, galley pumps, eutectic refrigerators, bilge pumps, toilets, etc.) wears out much quicker than they would on land.

(iv) Because of point (i) above, electrical things (eg. batteries, alternators, wind generators, solar panels, electric bilge pumps, electric anchor winches, water systems, electric toilets, electric refrigerators, etc.) give out much faster than mechanical things.

(v) Electronic things (e.g. instruments such as GPS, speed indicators, inverters, TVs, radios, autopilots, video players, microwave ovens, weather faxes, depth sounders, fancy regulators, voltage splitters, etc.) give out faster and more frequently than either electrical or mechanical things because they have more delicate bits like circuit boards.

(vi) A simple application of logic will tell you that things which are a combination of mechanical, electrical and electronic will give out fastest of all (e.g. autopilots, Lectrasans, watermakers, etc.)

(v) In the ocean, water gets in everywhere eventually. All boats leak, but I will qualify that statement lest some manufacturer thinks it is too sweeping. I accept that some new boats such as Swans and Etaps (and perhaps some others) don't leak when they are new because they are tested in a factory water bath and are fixed before they leave the factory. For other boats it is a lottery. New boats are less likely to leak than old boats. However, given time, sealants harden, rubber and neoprene gaskets harden, 'O' rings wear out, silicone lets go, and water gets in. If you think you'll be able to prevent it, you're living in "La La Land". An addendum to this rule is: An ocean voyage is the best way to locate leaks. Some boats never leak until they make an ocean voyage. Most leaks are in the deck or cabin house.

(vi) What the corrosive environment of salt air doesn't damage, the sun and wind will. Sunshine and salt crystals are more destructive together on synthetic sailcloth, and synthetic lines (ropes), than separately.

Remember that money can solve all of these problems.
You might ask the question that, starting out with a new boat and equipment, how much time will you have with things running reliably. You can be lucky or unlucky (like cars there are lemons amongst boats), but I would guess that most things in my lists above last at least two or three years with electronics going first. Some of the mechanical things may go reliably for up to twenty years. A solid state regulator set in resin on your alternator could last indefinitely (unfortunately, everyone wants a smart regulator these days!).

The choice of boats in the medium category is vast. *Trade-A-Boat* is full of examples for sale. Try to think strength. Steel may be good. Ferro may be good but you can't see what's under the cement. Aluminium may also be good. Glass reinforced plastic may be good. The strength may come from the shell thickness but you should be able to look at the interior structure for appropriate reinforcing. You are looking for stringers, ribs, bracing, bulkheads, floors, beam shelves, etc.

Virtually all types of construction will have these in them with the possible exception of cored GRP hulls. (The best construction in GRP boats has the bulkheads glassed to the hull and bolted as well or fixed in some way with glass lapping through the bulkhead. You'll be hard put to find it on most boats.) American manufacturers of GRP boats used to favour thick hulls with less stiffening than British manufacturers who prefer more stiffening with thinner shells. The smallest size which is practical would be something like an Australian GRP H28 or the New Zealand made H28. Put another way, the smallest size would need to be around five tons.

I know that it is possible to do this in much smaller boats. One fellow circumnavigated in a thirteen foot steel boat. He was single-handing, fortunately.

Designers refer to a thing called displacement length ratio. Once upon a time, it was considered that a cruising boat should have a D/L ratio of at least 400. These days, people cruise regularly in boats with a D/L ratio of less than 200. The D/L ratio doesn't tell the whole story. Short, fat, heavy boats will have much higher ratios than long, skinny, light boats.

Let's compare a 35 foot boat that weighs four tons with a 35 foot boat that weighs seven tons. They are basically the same size. The mast and rigs will weigh a similar amount although the rig may have to be bigger on the heavier boat. But there won't be that much difference in weight. Given 4 hp per ton, the seven-tonner will need 28 hp and the four-tonner 16 hp. The 16 hp engine will weigh considerably more than half the 28 hp engine. Not much saving there. The weight saving of the lighter boat would be less than the weight of a person for rig and engine. Let's say both have a 50% ballast ratio. For the four-tonner, that leaves two tons for the hull, deck, interior, engine, rig and sails and whatever other weights the designer has factored in. For the seven-tonner, we have three and a half tons (less a couple of hundred pounds for engine and rig) for all the same stuff. It doesn't take much thinking to realise that the seven-tonner can be stronger and carry more stuff especially in its tanks.

When you are looking at the specifications of a production boat, notice the weight or displacement of the boat, and the tank capacity.
It suits manufacturers to build light boats because they use less material and thus, cost less to build, so profit margins can be higher. "Y" factory building the four tonner will be able to undersell the seven tonner built by "Z" factory. Both have three cabins, eight bunks, a shower, microwave oven and all the trimmings. And the cheaper four-tonner sails like the clappers and always out-sails the seven-tonner. Who is going to sell more boats and make the most money for shareholders? The trend of manufacturers is to lighter and lighter boats because the profit margins are higher. With European builders using quite sophisticated production techniques, costs are reduced even further in the interests of competition.

World markets have been dominated by the French for some years as evidenced by the charter boat industry, once dominated by American companies such as *Morgan* and *CSY*. The style of boat developed for the charter industry has also come to dominate cruising boat design. There are similarities to cruising requirements but for charter boats think very short term. This means the accent is on comfort. Accommodation, hot water and bathrooms will have more importance than sailing performance, which will be more a result of light displacement than hull design. Hull design will be about *accommodation and not sailing*. There are usually no sea berths on charter boats. If you ask about lee cloths (a panel of heavy material such as sail cover stuff, designed to prevent you from falling out of the bunk when the vessel rolls) the salespeople won't know what you are talking about or they'll tell you their boats have everything. Be assured they won't have lee cloths or appropriate berths to put them on. They will have two or more showers including one on the stern to wash the salt off after emerging from the ocean. The bunks will all be doubles so charterers can enjoy their 'conjugals'. Some will have a large queen size double island berth in the spacious after cabin. They are designed to be safely at anchor at night. They are essentially <u>unsuitable</u> for medium and long term cruising unless significantly modified.

Unfortunately, because charter boats have such wonderful accommodation, people have started to require the same level in all boats regardless of length. To meet this demand, yacht manufacturers produce wider and wider hulls. To maintain lightness the hulls have to be very shallow and are thus quite flat on the bottom (dinghy style). The problem with this is that if they are heeled beyond a certain point they go right over and are stable upside down like a catamaran. For many modern designs, the angle at which the ability to right themselves vanishes is about 115 degrees (called the angle of vanishing stability). Twenty five degrees past a flat knockdown, they flip upside down and from that point require heeling over 65 degrees from the vertical before they self-right and flip back upright. These boats are not really suitable for crossing oceans. Many of them do cross quite safely, but you wouldn't catch me in one.

General Rule of the sea:

The more ocean miles you, do the more likely it is you will meet an ultimate storm. (Some folk are unlucky enough to meet one the first time they go out sailing – but this rare.)

Boats designed in the 1960s tended to have angles of vanishing stability at 135 to 145 degrees. Wave action alone was easy enough to flip them upright quickly following inversion. The factors which help stability are narrow hulls, high freeboard, deep keels, high ballast ratios (usually thirty-five percent or more), high bow and stern, and a large deckhouse or a raised deck.

There is also a ratio called the sail area/displacement ratio. This can vary from around 15 to over 20. A long skinny boat may go as high as 23. Joe Adams 'metre' designs are of this type. Short fat heavy boats would tend to have ratios in the order of 14 – 16. Commonly, ex-racing boats tend to have more sail area because they race in enclosed waters where the wind strengths are less. When ocean cruising, such boats are often most comfortable sailing with a reef in the mainsail and huge overlapping genoas are rarely used. Be aware that there is a lot of variation in wind strengths throughout the world. High latitudes generally have greater wind strength than the tropics. Cold air is denser or heavier. Southern California, USA, generally has lighter winds than Sydney, NSW.

Waters around Great Britain generally have stronger winds than either of the other two. Boats designed with these areas in the mind of the designer will have sail areas appropriate to the perceived average wind speed. Wind strengths are also seasonal with stronger winds being felt in winter. I use the term "generally", because I know tropical summers can produce tropical cyclones, hurricanes or typhoons with wind speeds of over 200 miles per hour. The sail area ratio is calculated on the area of the mainsail plus 100% of the area of the fore triangle. A boat with a sail area displacement ratio of less than fifteen has too little sail area and will be too slow in light conditions although it may be fine if you are intending sailing in the Great Southern Ocean. Interestingly, most boats in the cruising yacht size range tend to average around four to six knots on their ocean passages. There's not much in it.

Masts and Sails

To some people the words "ketch" and "schooner" are frightfully romantic. People think of Gardner McKay and his *Adventures in Paradise* (if they're old enough !). Here are some facts: One mast (sloop or cutter) costs less than two masts with all the rigging and sails and gear. There is a mathematical relationship between windward ability and luff length of sails. The sloop/cutter rig will out sail the ketch rig to windward on the same hull.

Here are some opinions: There is a limit to how much sail area a person can manage and age and fitness need to be taken into account. Consider the exercise of tying in an ordinary slab reef in a mainsail which has been left up too long in strengthening wind. In my opinion most folk can handle mainsails on boats to around 35 to 40 feet. Once the boats start to get over 40 feet the sails can become a bit of a handful and require some extra strength and fitness. I have found winching in a big genoa on a roller furler on a 45 footer in about Force 5/6, a gut buster. (I wasn't coughing blood, but it was hard work.) Clearly the mainsail will be smaller on a ketch than a sloop/cutter of the same size. So it seems reasonable that a ketch can be larger than a sloop yet still have sails of a manageable size. The more assistance one has to manage the sails e.g. large winches, large diameter furling drums, furling mainsails and furling headsails, then the larger those sails can be and still be manageable. Be aware that these things are not entirely foolproof and can break down, especially if given enough time. For mainsails, in-mast furling is more difficult to maintain than in-boom furling. Also remember that the more turning blocks and the like that a line passes through, the greater will be the effort required to overcome all the friction. This will be so where 'everything is led back to the cockpit'. Things with ball bearings and races will have less friction than things with plain bearings and bushes. However because of the marine environment the actual balls will be synthetic and subject to more wear (but not rust) than metal balls.

The schooner seems to be largely an American invention and was most likely designed for a particular set of conditions which suited that configuration. I would assume that those conditions involved a lot of off-the-wind or downwind sailing. 'Individualism' would be the only reason I could see for ever considering a schooner.

The yawl is a close relation of the ketch and was invented to give an advantage in some racing rule. It has nothing to recommend it. Adherents of this type of yacht will usually tell you how useful the mizzen mast is to hang stuff off like Radomes and wind generators. The Concordia Yawl is a famous American type which can send Americans into states of hypnotic reverie. They're okay if your taste runs to low freeboard, long counter sterns (somewhere to put the mizzen mast) and bow overhangs, narrow beam and relatively tight accommodation.

SPECIAL FEATURE:
DOWNWIND PASSAGEMAKING

SAILING DOWNWIND GOOSEWINGED LIKE THIS SCHOONER, THE AMERICANS CALL "READIN' BOTH PAGES"

The Americans also like the cat rig which has one enormous mainsail set on a mast (sometimes unstayed) right up in the bow. This rig is called the 'una' rig in the UK. The Laser dinghy is a modern version. Catboats in the USA traditionally have a short, wide, shallow hull. They were designed for operating in very shallow water and are useless for ocean sailing. In a blow, the rig will generate massive weather helm (the tendency of the boat to round up into the wind). The rig may have merit in ordinary hulls but I have never seen one. The Americans also produced the *Cat Ketch* (called a 'Periauger' by Howard Chappelle) which has two mainsails of equal size set on two masts. (The Freedom 40, and its derivatives, is of this type.)

In the general area of fore-and-aft rigged vessels, which includes all of the above, a single sail on a mast which extends forward of the mast as well as behind the mast is called a lug sail. There are three types of lugsails. The 'dipping lugsail' is an old English type and has no place on a cruising boat. The other two types of lugsails are of the balanced type. The standing lugsail has a spar along the top edge of the sail and a boom along its bottom edge. Both spars extend either side of the mast with the smaller area of sail being ahead of the mast. When the wind is on one side of the boat the sail presses against the mast and when the wind is on the other side the sail pulls away from the mast. It is generally only found in smaller vessels, some dinghies and traditional boats, generally from the south-west part of the UK.

The other type of standing balanced lugsail is the traditional Chinese lugsail, characterised by a number full length battens across the sail. There are a lot of regional variations in this type. Western yachts with Chinese lugsails usually owe their development to Jock McLeod and Blondie Hasler if from the UK, and Tom Colvin if from the USA. There are many who swear by this type of rig. It has the advantage of being extremely cheap. You don't even need sailcloth as any material will do (except netting!). The masts are mostly unstayed so there is little rigging, and since the ropes are lightly loaded they can be cheap sisal or any natural fibre. You are in the realm of real shoestring cruising if you choose to go low-tech Chinese lugsail. They do not sail as close to the wind as Bermudan types but they are often faster off the wind. They will not heave to but they are easier to reef than any other type. Chinese lugsails are more suited to vessels which are not too beamy. They also work well on shoal draft vessels. (Tom Colvin's Gazelle design is a good example of a boat designed for this type of rig.) The Folkboat, *Jester*, sailed in most of the singlehanded transatlantic races by Blondie Hasler, and later by Mike Richey, was set up with a single Chinese lugsail so you didn't have to go on deck for anything (except anchoring or tying up!). Both Richey and Hasler boasted of making the Atlantic crossing in slippers!

At the other extreme are Carbospars Aerorig which is extremely high tech and most likely costs a king's ransom compared with aluminium and stainless steel equivalents. I suspect you get your money's worth but longevity has yet to be determined.

You may come across gaff and gunter rigs. Both of these have a spar attached to the top edge of the sail which is hoisted up the mast. With the gunter rig, when the sail is set, the spar is virtually an extension of the mast. An example of a boat which may have a gunter rig is the Eventide 24/26. A gaff rig has more ropes to pull and play with than Bermudan or Marconi rigs (which is what we call the set-up on most vessels these days). Advantages of gaff rigs are: faster off the wind than Bermudan rigs, lower centre of effort of sails (therefore less heeling), shorter mast for under bridges etc., low tech, mainsail drops instantly because of the weight of the spar, greater sail area. The disadvantages are: not as good to windward as Bermudan rigs, more subject to chafe and wear, more weather helm when reefed, more complicated especially if topsails used, lots of rope needed, low tech. Gaff rigs are a powerful rig and were used for fishing boats which towed trawls and the like. They are probably better suited for relatively shallow draft boats than tall Bermudan rigs.

There are various other forms of rigs which come and go, including ones with solid sails (wings on end), the Gallant rig, and other inventions, which enjoyed some brief passing interest before entering history. Experimental rigs probably aren't appropriate for your first cruising boat.

In modern terminology, the sloop has one sail in front of the mast and the cutter has two sails in front of the mast. I will leave out spinnakers, bloopers, MPSs, drifters and other light wind sails. Headsails are attached to stays either by sail hanks or a luff groove in a roller furling tube. The outermost forestay is attached to the top of the mast (in a masthead rig) in both sloops and cutters. The cutter has an inner forestay attached somewhere down the mast. The disadvantage of a cutter is that to balance the pull of the inner forestay on the mast there must be stays aft of the mast. Because of the boom, the stays, called runners, must be able to be released and tensioned easily. A way to solve this is to have the inner forestay connected close to the spreaders where the load can be taken by aft lower shrouds (if fitted). The masthead cutter rig is the most versatile of single-masted rigs. I regard it as the best for shorthanded ocean sailing for vessels under 40 feet. As the wind increases, sail areas can be progressively reduced, whilst still retaining sail balance with less sail changing than on a sloop.

Some yachts do not have the forestay going to the top of the mast. These boats are called fractional rigged. If the forestay is quite near the top it might be called seven-eighths or fifteen-sixteenths. If well down the mast it might be called three quarters. Fractional rigs are more complicated than masthead rigs and were developed for some racing advantage. By having a bit of free standing mast, the mainsail can be easily flattened for stronger winds by tightening the backstay, which bends the top of the mast and so flattens the sail. The problem is that by working the mast in this way you are increasing the likelihood that it will fracture sooner than if it were stayed at the masthead. Older vessels were often fractionally rigged and had jumper struts and diamond stays sticking out where the forestay is attached to the mast. This eliminates the need for runners. An example of this type of rig can be found on the 22' Bluebird.

Full length battens provide mainsails with a better shape and thus they sail better. Also, they don't flog. However, they are more prone to chafe. You can have a mainsail without any battens at all, but it needs to have a slight hollow cut in the leach (back edge of the sail) and will therefore be of less sail area than it would have been with battens. I have heard this called a Swedish Mainsail. The problem with battens is that they chafe on the stays and against the sail. (Sails chafe on stays but it is not as localised as when battens are fitted.) For long term cruising, being without battens altogether may be the best option. If you are long term cruising then you won't be in a hurry so you won't miss a bit of sail area. Full length battens work with either boom furling or slab reefing. If a sail has to have battens then I'd make them full length as the advantages far outweigh the disadvantages.

In summary, depending on your fitness, I'd reckon on one mast on boats up to around forty feet and two masts on boats over 45 feet. It will depend on whether you have roller reefing and boom furling and how easy it is to grind the sails in when the wind starts to blow. I am assuming it is a normal two person crew. In this arrangement, one person keeps an eye on things while the other does the sail reduction. Once you have more than two crew, circumstances may be different. The most common cruising crew comprises a man and his partner (who may or may not be his wife – but that is of no concern here, and in fact, once cruising you'll find nobody gives a fig whether it's a couple of girls, a couple of blokes, or a chap and his mother – acceptance reigns). The fact is that if you're old enough to have retired from work and you're not all that fit, then a thirty-five footer may be what you can manage best. There's another reason for that, which I'll mention later.

Sails and Rigging
The racing influence tends to have mainsails with two slab reefing points. They seem to have about three feet reduction in luff length with each reef. On a cruising boat, the first reef is a waste of time. It takes a fair amount of effort to put in a reef. I wouldn't waste my time with a first reef (unless you've a full crew who love going on deck to reef sails). Go straight to the second reef if the wind starts to get up. You'll be far more comfortable. Get your sailmaker to put in a third row of reefing eyes and cringles at least six or eight feet above the second reef. Then with the third reef in you'll have a sail area comparable to a trysail and, if your sail is of fairly robust material, you won't need a trysail. Another way of estimating the depth of the third reef is, if your boat has single spreaders then with the third reef tied in, the top of the sail should be a little above the spreaders. If your boat has two sets of spreaders then with the third reef in, the top of the sail should be one third to half way between the two sets of spreaders. If the wind increases further, then the next sail reduction will be to drop the mainsail altogether and sail on storm jib alone. A triple reefed mainsail and storm jib should probably handle around thirty-five to forty knots. Boom furling allows infinite amounts of sail reduction.

Sails used to be made out of cotton/canvas and being from a natural fibre were subject to rot or decomposition. Then along came the synthetic material Dacron (which is a trade name) or terylene. Sails made of this wonder material are subject to sun degradation and chafe but they can be repaired and restitched and last for years. A sail could last ten years easily on a full time cruising boat. Mylars, Kevlars and laminated sails are a waste of money on a cruising yacht. If you like to do a bit of racing as well, I guess it's a different story. I think it was AEsop who wrote that a fool and his money are soon parted. It's still true and never more so than in boats. Coloured sails don't make as much glare as white sails in bright sunlight but they are usually dearer. Dacron/terylene is the cheapest sail material and other exotic types such as Duradon are for specific purposes.

General Rule for People: If you have a flashy personality then you'll buy whatever it takes to be noticed.

You are going to need a proper storm jib. If it can be set from an inner forestay then you'll have snug rig under storm jib only for winds up to about force twelve. Remember that if your boat was used for racing at some stage then the chances are that the storm jib, if it has one, will be too large.

(Those racing types just can't help themselves!) If your boat is around thirty feet long then your storm jib should be no more than 50 square feet and around a maximum of 80 square feet for a forty-footer. A trysail is nice, but they are a bit of a pain to set. With a trysail, the boom is not used and must be tied down out of the way. Some boats have a separate trysail track on the mast because otherwise you'd have to remove the main from the mast track. Time spent fiddling around on deck in a blow should be kept to a minimum.

Roller Furling Headsails really are a wonderful invention. They beat sitting up to your waist in water when the bow buries in a wave as you undo sail hanks and bundle up headsails. Some headsail furling systems are quite sophisticated and others are thoroughly agricultural. Generally, money = sophistication + brand name. Note, as mentioned above, big headsails can require quite an effort to roll in even using a multi-speed winch. If you have decided on a roller furling headsail, measure the diameter of your forestay and replace it with one which is one or two sizes bigger before you fit/buy your furler. Furlers put a lot of sideways strain on the ends of the forestay where the swages are. You will need a stronger stay. It will also be a good time to fit twin backstays. Just for the extra precaution and you can incorporate your HF radio aerial in one (ask the rigger to fit insulators). Commercial ceramic electricity insulators used in the electricity industry are safer (the loops of wire intersect) and cheaper but they only seem to make them in large sizes in Australia.

Major Robert Fiennes Wykeham-Martin invented sail furling (not reefing) equipment in the 1890s. It is permanently attached to a wire luff headsail and works. Top swivels and bottom drums are still made in bronze and come in three sizes. They can be obtained from Davies in the UK.

Rigging Wire is usually stainless steel of type 304. Some of it is 316 but that is rarer and more expensive. The two types have different corrosion properties. The construction is comprised of nineteen strands twisted together. This is called 1 by 19. There are types which are flattened on the outside to be smoother and more wind resistant (called Dyform). Racing boats use solid drawn stainless called rod rigging. It can be smaller in diameter than 1 by 19 for the same amount of stainless and is thus less wind resistant. Racing sailors are fanatical about that. I suppose if you add up the length of all the wire in the rigging and take off a fraction of the diameter and multiply it by the length of all the stays, you might have a reduction of a few square inches or perhaps a square foot or two. If you remember my point about things breaking, all rigging will eventually break because it works. The problem with rod rigging is that when one strand breaks, that's it, because there is only one strand. You'll lose your mast and the lot. Unless you can afford to replace all your rod rigging each year, leave it to the racers. Rod rigging has no place on a cruising yacht. There are two other types of stainless wire found on yachts. Wire which is of 7 by 19 construction is more flexible than 1 by 19 and is used for halyards and sometimes lifelines. Wire is used because it has less stretch than rope. This is no big deal on a cruising boat. I'd personally prefer all rope halyards and not part rope/part wire as some have. Invariably some strands of wire break and stick out causing "meat hooks" which will leave blood on your deck. Besides, it's easier to end for end rope halyards to even out the wear. Some boats have 7 X 7 construction wire. This is more flexible/more stretchy than 1 by 19, less flexible/less stretchy than 7 X 19. You can use 7 X 7 in place of 1 by 19 to hold your mast up. It is quite easy to work in sizes up to 6mm using Talurit swages.

Some people like to use galvanised wire as it is less subject to work hardening and subsequent fracture than stainless wire. It needs to be treated every year so that it doesn't rust away. I regard this as just extra work for something that is not all that much cheaper than stainless.

Keels and Rudders

Long Keel or Fin Keel arguments have been around for about 100 years. There are pros and cons for both sides. A fin-keeled yacht has less wetted surface area and therefore less skin friction, meaning that it will be easier to push through the water at slow speeds than a boat of the same waterline length with more wetted surface area. Manufacturers prefer fin keels because they use less material and are cheaper to make (= more profit), the sailing is more responsive and they turn more quickly and manoeuvre better under power. Those who prefer long keels claim they are steadier on the helm, easier to make self-steering, give protection to the rudder and are stronger as they provide a backbone to the boat.

I would offer two pieces of advice: Firstly, many places in the world, because of their tidal range have grids for cleaning and antifouling your yacht. Your boat sits on the grid as the tide goes out and is tied fore and aft to posts. If the base of the keel is long enough for the boat to stand on unsupported without toppling forward or backwards then the fin keel is okay by me. Secondly if, when the boat is sitting on its fin keel, you can induce movement (flexing) of the hull by pulling or pushing on bow or stern, then I wouldn't buy that boat for ocean cruising. Remember that a fin-keel is a big lump of lead or cast iron that is attached to the hull over quite a small area. I would want to know that it was very well supported inside, both across the hull (by floors) and lengthways (by stringers). Imagine the hull on its side, say hanging from a crane, there's a couple of tons of lead sticking out – think of the bending forces on those close-together keel bolts.

Rudders come in different forms. Originally, rudders were attached to the back edge of the keel. To reduce wetted surface area designers moved the rudder further forward and raked it. The more this happened, the less responsive rudders became. Then the rudder was separated from the keel and placed further towards the stern so that it was more effective in turning the boat. In most GRP boats the rudder has a stainless steel shaft running through the hull (sometimes the shaft is hollow, sometimes it is made from exotics such as carbon fibre). It is supported in the hull by a top and bottom bearing (or bush – preferably not nylon as it expands in water). The top may emerge into the cockpit and have a tiller fitted or under the cockpit floor it may have a quadrant fitted so it can be steered by a steering wheel set on a pedestal in the cockpit.

Under the water the rudder shaft has flanges welded to it and it is covered in glass, foam, wood, whatever, and glassed over and faired. The rudder pivots about the shaft to steer the boat. If there is some area of rudder in front of the shaft the rudder is said to be "balanced," in that the area in front of the rudder helps to turn the rudder. Some boats have a fixed part of the hull (a skeg) in front of the rudder, which extends for all or part of the depth of the rudder. The skeg may have a lower bearing to support the rudder. Older boats and boats with full length keels had the rudder hanging off the stern supported by gudgeons and pintles. Some modern boats have this also (Northshore 33). Rudders tend not to give any trouble although the bearings may need replacing after ten or more years. If the boat suffers a grounding, the rudder shaft may become bent and need straightening. A rudder hanging off the stern is much easier to work on than one through the hull which has to be dropped down (into a ditch?) to be removed for working on. A rudder which is only supported by hull bearings and not a skeg should have a fairly hefty shaft. Lloyds Insurers in London produce *Rules for Yacht Construction.* Get yourself a copy and have a look at the rudder shaft diameter recommendations. For an unpleasant surprise, then go and measure the rudder shaft diameters on a few yachts.

In a yacht steered by a quadrant under the floor and a wheel on a pedestal, a large wheel is a nuisance as it is hard to get past. Racing yachts like to have large wheels (sometimes called a destroyer wheel). There are several possible reasons for this. (a) the steering is fairly direct and a large wheel is needed to supply the effort to turn the rudder or (b) the boat has lots of weather helm and needs a big wheel for the extra effort required to hold the yacht on course or (c) a large wheel allows the helmsman to sit well out to the side of the boat to see better or (d) simple ostentation. Some racing yachts are wide enough to have two wheels so the helmsman can steer from either side. I guess because everyone drives a car, they want to steer with a wheel. Perhaps people just don't have the physical ability and coordination to adapt to tillers. The tiller is a perfectly good way to steer a boat. You can sit sideways and brace yourself with your feet, you can apply great strength to the tiller with your torso, and a tiller is a much simpler device than wheels with their quadrants, wires, chains or hydraulics. It is far less likely to break down in some remote place.

Some vintage yachts were wheel steered and used a curved rack and pinion on the top of the rudder shaft (Edson Steering). If kept greased this type of steering seems to last forever.

Diesel or Petrol Engines
In the modern yacht the lightweight diesel engine rules. Diesel fumes do not ignite by spark or naked flame in the way that petrol does and so it is safer to have on board in enclosed spaces. Petrol fumes are heavier than air and will gather in the bilge waiting for the fool with the cigarette lighter or the candle. Diesel and petrol engines are heat engines of the internal combustion type. (A steam engine is an external combustion heat engine.) Diesel engines have higher compression ratios than petrol engines because they use the heat of compression to ignite the distillate/air mixture. (Petrol engines use a spark plug.) The greater stresses of a diesel engine require that it be stronger than other types of engines. Diesel engines develop their maximum turning power (torque) at lower revolutions than petrol engines. Being slower and stronger than petrol engines, diesels tend to last longer. They also use much less fuel as they extract more power from it. Other than a need for electric starting, diesels do not require electricity to run. If you can get air and fuel to them they will run underwater.

(Some of you may have noticed diesel four wheel drive vehicles with snorkels running up beside the windscreen – this is for crossing moderately deep rivers. A snorkel on a petrol 4WD is idiotic when you realise what it's for. Ostentation or fools and their money?)

Because of the dominance of diesel engines, there are now few petrol inboard motors available. There are a lot of old brands around like Albin, Stuart Turner, and in the USA just about every yacht before 1970 had an Atomic Four. You can import a Vire (7 or 12 hp) or an RCA Dolphin (12 or 16 hp), and Blaxland Chapman and Hardman and Hall Simplex engines are still made, I believe. But these are engines for smallish boats (although the side valve Simplex is a pretty hefty object).

Internal combustion engines are two-stroke or four-stroke. Most diesels are four-stroke although GM Detroit make a two stroke diesel, but you won't find these in the sort of yachts I'm talking about. The two-stroke petrol engine was probably designed to use fuel faster than it can be pumped out of the ground. But they are the smallest, lightest and most powerful type of engine. Until recently most outboard engines were two-strokes. Heavier (and more expensive) four-stroke outboards have become more popular lately because they are less polluting. Two-stroke engines tend not to run at idling speeds very well whereas four strokes can idle all day.

Some outboards are made with low geared propellers to push large boats – such as houseboats – at slowish speeds. Such motors are alternatives for yachts. The advantage of an outboard is that it can be taken off the boat to be worked on in comfort or sent away to be worked on. If it hangs over thetern or is in a well, the petrol can be kept clear of the accommodation. There is also the advantage that not much goes wrong with a petrol engine that the average yacht owner can't fix himself. However, servicing a diesel fuel pump and injectors at Suvarov Atoll may be beyond the ability of the average cruising man. Outboards cost less in initial purchase than inboards. Yamaha make a diesel outboard, I think, but these are really heavy. A company in Italy named Carniti, also used to make diesel outboards.

The secret of trouble free two-stroke engines is clean spark plugs. The secret of trouble free diesel engines is clean fuel.

Engine Cooling can be of three types. Air cooling is less common but Yamaha make an industrial diesel which is air cooled and on older yachts you may find Ducati air-cooled diesels up to about 16 hp and some Lister diesels were also air-cooled in 8, 16 and 24hp ratings. The problem with air-cooled engines is that they are hot and they need to have cool air drawn in from outside and hot air expelled outside. Ducting is needed. Air-cooled engines are also noisier than liquid cooled engines.

Generally, purpose-built marine engines are raw water cooled – they use sea water drawn in from outside and expelled with the exhaust. There are not many brands of purpose built marine engines now available. Each of the Scandinavian countries has their own brand – Bukh from Denmark, Volvo from Sweden and Sabb from Norway. I have no experience of them but some people believe Sabb is the pick. Germany used to make Farymann but Perkins bought them out. These are a superior engine. Yanmar is from Japan and Lister is from the UK.

Many makes of engines are converted industrial engines and may have dissimilar metals in their construction hence they do not use raw sea water for cooling. From Japan come Isuzu, Kubota, Mitsubishi, Toyota and Nissan. Daewoo are from Korea, Hatz are from Germany, and CMC are from China. There are lots of others. Most of these engines can be identified by having heat exchangers attached to them. The engines are cooled by fresh water in a closed system which is in turn cooled by raw sea water drawn in from outside the hull and expelled with the exhaust. Two pumps are required – one circulates the water in the engine and the other circulates the sea water through the heat exchanger. (Raw water cooled engines only use one water pump.)

The alternative to a heat exchanger is a keel cooler. Here the engine coolant is circulated through a pipe outside the hull and is cooled by the sea water flowing past the pipe. The water must flow from aft forwards through the pipe. The size and length of the pipe is critical but can be surprisingly small and create little drag. It is a simple foolproof system requiring only one pump and it is a pity that it is not more widely used. If the external pipe is fractured then salt water replaces the fresh water and the engine continues to run.

Anchors and Anchoring

If you are going cruising then you'll need more than one anchor. Most cruising yachts use plow anchors. CQR is the brand name of Simpson Lawrence of Glasgow, Trevco and Highwood are Australian brand names, Manson is a New Zealand brand name. There are also sand anchors. Danforth is a USA brand name as is Fortress. Other anchor types are Bruce anchors (a type and a brand name) and, increasingly of late, Delta anchors (a brand name from Simpson Lawrence). There are other lesser known types. All these anchors are known as "lightweight" anchors to distinguish hem from Dreadnought, Fisherman, Admiralty pattern, Herreschoff pattern, and some other type anchors.

For lightweight anchors, the standard was a minimum of one pound of anchor for each foot of length. So the main anchor (sometimes called the bower anchor) for a 45 footer should be at least 45 lbs weight or more. The thing that joins the anchor to the boat is called the anchor rode and it can be a mixture of chain and rope or all chain. If chain and rope then it is considered that there must be a minimum of ten metres of chain. For anchor chain a rough guide to size is, if over 40 feet then have half inch (12 mm) chain, 30 to 40 feet have three eighths (10 mm) chain, 20 to 30 feet have five sixteenths (8 mm) chain and under 20 feet quarter inch (6 mm) chain. The other end of the rope should be attached to a U-bolt or some other strong point inside the boat so you don't lose the lot if it all runs out. If you have an all chain rode then there should be ten or more feet of heavy nylon on the end which attaches to the boat. This will absorb the shock if all your chain runs out. Two hundred feet of fast running half inch chain could easily rip out a strong U-bolt. The other reason for having nylon at the end is that if you have to get away in a hurry and don't have time to retrieve your anchor you can cut the line easily to let the lot go. It may be a better alternative than losing your boat. The anchor rode breaking strain needs to be substantial, say a minimum one ton or more for a thirty-footer, up to maybe four tons or more for a forty-footer. Nylon is stronger than silver rope but may be less abrasion resistant.

When anchoring, the ratio of amount of rode out to depth of water, should be in the order of seven to one for shallowish anchorages, through to a minimum of three to one in very deep anchorages. You will need to have some regard for the other boats already anchored because the convention is that if two boats start to bump, the boat which anchored last is the one that has to up-anchor and leave.

You need a minimum of two anchors regardless of what sort of cruising you are doing. Three or four anchors are more sensible for medium to long term cruising. You should have at least one other anchor equivalent to your main anchor set up with a rope and chain or all chain rode. You should have the makings of at least three full sets of anchoring equipment. Your anchor may be the most important safety device on your boat. Some boats carry seven anchors or more.

Retrieving your anchor may be the time when you regret having a 45-footer with a sixty pound plow and all chain rode, with your batteries flat. There you are on the foredeck coughing blood, eyes blinded with sweat and a juicy hernia growing in your trousers. It's hardly the time to regret not buying that thirty-two footer that seemed ideal, but cost far less than the allocated budget. I reckon the size of boat should be governed by the weight of chain and anchor you can lift. If you must have a powered anchor winch, then, when the electric winch motor has burned out or the batteries are flat, you also need a length of line and chain hook, which can be attached to the anchor rode at deck level and taken back to a sheet winch. You re-attach the line to the rode at the bow each time the bight of rode reaches the sheet winch; simple, but test out how it works before you have to use it in anger. A manual anchor winch will be more reliable but slower than an electric winch. Remember that electric anchor winches should only be used when the engine is running.

Stoves
Stoves can run on gas (propane, butane or Compressed Natural Gas), alcohol (methylated spirits), kerosene (paraffin), diesel or anything combustible such as white spirit, driftwood or coal. Butane is a liquid at much lower pressures than propane and is commonly found in camping type stoves that use disposable gas canisters. Propane gas bottles are much stronger and are filled from service stations and the like. The gas bottles have a ten year life and need pressure retesting after that. Most gas bottles will rust in the marine environment but stainless steel ones are made. If they only have a ten year life then galvanised gas bottles may be the more economical proposition. Gas stoves are simple to use and operate but, unless purpose built for the marine environment, can rust out quickly. Gas is heavier than air and the same precautions which apply to petrol apply to gas, except for CNG which is lighter than air and safest of all, but is expensive to install and not readily available throughout the world.

Kerosene has poor heating ability so kero stoves use vaporising burners which have to be pre-heated with another fuel such as alcohol. They can be quite troublesome with flare-ups, burners that need regular pricking and sooty flames. However, kerosene is a cheap, widely available fuel. Alcohol stoves are very safe because alcohol mixes with water and its fire is easily extinguished. Alcohol is many times more expensive than kero in poorer countries because, even though it has been poisoned with wood alcohol (methyl alcohol), people like to drink it. Alcohol stoves have a fairly high consumption of alcohol relative to kerosene in kero stoves so they are not that cheap to run. Diesel stoves are wonderful in colder climates and use the same cheap fuel as the boat's engine, making them the most economical of all. They are not available in Australia, so you'd have to import one from Canada. There may be an importer in Tasmania.

Refrigeration
Refrigeration on yachts is of two main types. One type uses the same principles as your refrigerator at home. It has a sealed unit compressor driven by a 12 volt electric motor. A cooling plate in the insulated box keeps the temperature at a set level by means of a thermostat.

The other type of refrigeration uses a car air-conditioning compressor driven by belts off the main engine. Refrigerant is circulated through a plate (called a eutectic plate) in the insulated compartment. The plate freezes and keeps the contents cool as it slowly thaws. The engine is run as often as needed to keep the temperature low in the fridge. Some yachts have portable fridges which run off electricity or kerosene quite efficiently and there are small solid state fridges (heat or cool) which seem to use electricity very inefficiently.

In this modern day, we have UHT Long Life milk, tinned butter and Cryovac meat. You probably shouldn't eat too much meat anyway but there are salamis and other preserved forms of meat that don't require refrigeration. Refrigeration is one of the most unreliable devices found on yachts. In any anchorage there are always lots of yachts with faulty refrigeration. My advice would be to have refrigeration by all means but don't rely on it and be prepared to throw lots of rotting food over the side. I would suggest that there are very few really long-term cruising people who are bothered with refrigeration.

Self-Steering
A person could just about write a book on each of the topics I've chosen and a number of books have been written on self-steering. Everyone these days seems to want highly sophisticated, computerised self-steering with electric motors driving hydraulic pumps and rams attached to the rudder shaft. This stuff costs bulk money, it uses electricity and it breaks down. Other sailors can't live without their Aries windvane and servo pendulum self-steering, or perhaps it's a Monitor, or Sailomat, or Haslar, or Gunning, or QME, or Fleming, or any one of a dozen or more different varieties that cost a small fortune to buy and have bearings that seize and wear, bits that break, and bits that corrode.

Buy if you wish – I've talked about money before, but you don't actually need all that stuff. By trimming your sails and using a sheet-to-tiller system, you can sail on course for thousands of miles without touching anything. Joshua Slocum did it. Sadly, people just don't believe me. They think it's some sort of magic which they are incapable of performing on their boat. People have allowed themselves into being brainwashed into thinking that they couldn't possibly sail on the ocean without a bloody great collection of pipes and metal hanging off the stern of their yacht. I put it down to no confidence in themselves, no initiative, herd mentality and too much money. Besides how can anyone recognise a real cruising boat if it doesn't have self-steering?

I believe that most of the mechanical windvane self-steering gears available these days have most of the bugs worked out. A lot of long-term cruising types report favourably on Aries. Windvane types aren't much good for motoring (or steaming). Electronic self-steering is best for this as your engine is generating enough power to drive the device. If you are really keen, you can set a small low powered electronic tiller actuated unit (Autohelm or Navic) on the servo pendulum actuating arm of your mechanical self-steering gear and steer the boat under sail or power.

Unfortunately, electronic self-steering pilots are probably the most unreliable widely available devices ever invented for yachts. Open one up and you'll find tiny little plastic gearwheels and flimsy bits which certainly don't engender confidence in the reliability of the gadget. I suppose they're okay if used sparingly in calm water when motoring.

Dinghies

In dinghies, the choice is between inflatables and hard dinghies. One dark night I put my yacht on a lee shore sand bar on a falling tide. The plywood dinghy was thrown over the side and an anchor rowed quickly out into deep water. Time was of the essence. We managed to winch ourselves off in about fifteen minutes. In fifteen minutes I would have only just finished pumping up the inflatable and putting in the seats. Inflatables don't row well and don't row well to windward. That experience has convinced me that a hard dinghy is essential for serious cruising.

I also don't think you should put too much effort into maintaining your dinghy. People pinch dinghies and they will nearly always pinch the spiffy dinghy in preference to the crappy one. For pinching, inflatables are favoured over hard dinghies except if the dinghy is aluminium and then it is favoured most of all.

A hard dinghy should be as large as the crew is able to manhandle on and off the deck. Too small and fitting all the crew in becomes a trial if you're anchored a long way offshore. Finding the perfect dinghy is as hard as finding the perfect yacht. Some small catamaran or cathedral hulled dinghies are very stable and row and motor very well although they tend to be a little heavy. Pram types are the best load carriers. Dinghies need to have metal strips on the bottom so they can be dragged over rocks, sand, etc.

Inflatable dinghies come in a variety of types. The donut has an air tube all around it. A special bracket is used for the outboard. Some have a timber transom for mounting the outboard and some have a rigid fibreglass bottom. Inflatable dinghies are made out of nylon material which has a layer of water impervious substance calendared onto each side. The combinations are Hypalon/Hypalon, Hypalon/Neoprene, and modified PVC/PVC. Many of the more modern brands are of this latter construction. PVC, accelerated by the sun ultimately hardens and cracks away from the material. But modified PVC dinghies haven't been around long enough to see what the expected age may be. Some of the Hypalon types have lasted thirty years so far. If you look at it from the manufacturers' point of view, you'll see that PVC is cheaper (with the possibility for greater profit margins) and if lasts ten years, nobody will mind paying for a replacement, hence they can sell more boats. So, if you were an inflatable manufacturer, wouldn't you switch to PVC ?

Outboards

It's enormous fun to scream through the anchorage with a ten or fifteen horsepower outboard on your dinghy. Even more fun since it's illegal in Australia without a licence and boat registration. So, if you are cruising, what's the need for the hurry. If you feel a need to rush everywhere I'd say you shouldn't be cruising.

The perfect outboard can be raised over your head with one arm. This limits you to around two horsepower (cheaper to buy, cheaper to run). If you can't lift it with one arm then there's a strong likelihood you'll overbalance at some stage and give your motor a dunking, maybe even lose it if the anchorage is deep. If the yacht you choose has davits on the stern and you can leave the outboard on the dinghy, then you could get by with a slightly larger outboard say up to 6 hp. If your crew has more than two people, then the outboard size can go up accordingly with the size of the dinghy. It all comes down to money. If you've got lots, buy whatever you like but you don't need it.

Arthur Bieser, who wrote a book in the 60s or 70s called *The Proper Yacht,* used a five hp British Seagull to power his dinghy and also to move his 45' engineless yacht, *Minots Light*, around anchorages.

Multihulls

I have little experience of multihulls. The last one I sailed on was a Hobie 16 in about 25 knots of wind. The experience was exhilarating. Multihull aficionados are different to monohull sailors, perhaps as a result of long years defending their craft. Advocates for multihulls will tell you that they sail faster and flatter. You can leave a glass of your favourite beverage on the cabin table and it won't have tipped over hours later. Catamarans with bridge deck accommodation are very big on space. A thirty five foot bridge deck catamaran will have more accommodation than a 45 foot monohull. The great beam of catamarans makes them very hard to tip over. They don't carry tons of lead or iron ballast making them easy to be unsinkable. So, if you lost your mast and holed one of the hulls, the result would not necessitate abandonment. They have a great range of inverted stability and can float for years in this position (so too, can some recently designed monohulls.) Catamarans do not like being too heavily loaded. Some cruising cats are not as close winded as monos. With their shallow draft they are well suited to shoal waters cruising. Also they can be easily beached for maintenance. The main problem with catamarans in Australia is that they are very expensive. I would guess the best way to get one would be to build it yourself. Choose a design and have a good look at others of the type before committing yourself.

Trimarans are the sports cars of yachting. Owning one shows a single minded devotion to the God speed. They are not particularly roomy and you can't put too much stuff in them, but they are quick. They can be unsinkable, they float comfortably inverted, they're easily beached and they sail flatter than a monohull. Only a small outboard is needed. There are some old plywood types around from the days of Hedley Nichols and Arthur Piver and others. Ian Farrier seems to design the only production types around these days. If you like to travel light then a tri may suit you for long term cruising.

Safety

There are two schools of thought on the subject of safety. The late Eric Hiscock (he died in bed) believed that it was your decision to go out on the big ocean and you shouldn't expect anyone else to risk their lives rescuing you from the situation you got yourself into; something about taking responsibility for your own actions. Now that's really old-fashioned thinking. Who takes responsibility for their own actions these days? Certainly the politicians don't, bureaucrats don't (although it is significant that both these groups talk a lot about accountability), people who run the big businesses don't (limited liability, remember?), so why should sailors. Get with the flow. The cruising yacht may be the last refuge of the rugged individualist. There are still many people out there sailing who agree with Eric Hiscock.

The other school of thought on safety, the 'authorities', the bureaucrats, the safety organisations, the people who organise and administer yacht racing, believe in passive rescue. You power up your electrical devices and sit and wait for the cavalry to come to your aid. The individualists believe in self-aid. You save yourself. The first line of defence is prevention. You develop skills and experience – you pay attention, study and learn. You use jackstays and harnesses. You set out in a boat that is suitable and properly prepared for every emergency contingency. The boat may be unsinkable even if half stove in by a container or a whale. You carry spares, you know how to repair everything. There isn't any part of your boat you don't know. Even if you end up abandoning your yacht, your dinghy/raft/Carley float will be able to be sailed to safety with you living from your grab bag and raw fish.

So, what do I reckon is the ideal cruising boat for a couple?
It would be around 35 feet long and about seven or eight tons displacement, masthead sloop rigged with an inner forestay to set a storm jib on, and a simple boat without refrigeration. It would have a manual anchor winch and mechanical self-steering, or tiller steering. I'd carry a hard dinghy and a 2 hp outboard and possibly an inflatable as a spare.

***

Lin and Larry Pardey, in their first cruising book, advised "Go small, go simple, go now." That advice still holds true. Keep within what you can afford and don't load yourself down with money-wasting paraphernalia. Sterling Hayden, another great sailor, wrote that a person can become buried "beneath a pyramid of time payments and useless gadgetry. The years thunder by and the dreams of youth lie caked in dust on the shelves of patience. Before you know it the tomb is sealed."

Life isn't a trial run. If you want to go, just ***go for it.***

About the Author

Bruce W Walker grew up in Sydney, part of a large and gregarious family. Like many people of his generation with parents affected by the Great Depression, he chose a career in the Public Service – in particular, teaching. By the time he entered teacher training, he was dreaming of sailing boats. And it was during Bruce's teacher training that he met the love of his life, Cynthia.

Later, Bruce went back to university, where he trained in psychology to become a school counsellor. At university, he became firm friends with Greg Coonan.

Cynthia has been lover, wife, mother to their three children (Douglas, Brian and Jane) and sailing mate as well as best friend for decades. She provided both material and emotional support for all Bruce's sailing projects, including the designing and building of *Aragunnu*.

It is only in their later years when health problems interfered, that Cynthia has not participated in sailing with Bruce. Instead, they bought motorcycles to continue their love of outdoor adventure, and their daughter, Jane, races with Bruce or on her own in the twilight sailing races at Drummoyne Sailing club.

Bruce and Cynthia have been long-term members of the Coastal Cruising Club of Australia Inc. and been involved with the club committee for so many years, Bruce was awarded the honour of life membership. For many years, he edited the club's monthly magazine, *The Mainsheet*.

Bruce still avidly reads sailing books and magazines about sailing expeditions and ocean cruising. Now he has put together his own writings on the subject.

Acknowledgements

Thank you to Cynthia, lover, wife, partner and companion who has shared so many of my adventures and who has always been there to say, "Why not? Do it" in answer to the madcap ideas that I've come up with.

Thanks also to my friend and editor, Jan Mitchell, who provided encouragement, support, help and advice to make this book possible.